PRECUT
PATCHWORK PARTY

Creative Publishing
international

Copyright © 2013 Creative Publishing international, Inc.

First published in the United States of America by
Creative Publishing international, Inc., a member of
Quayside Publishing Group
400 First Avenue North
Suite 300
Minneapolis, MN 55401
1-800-328-3895
www.creativepub.com

ISBN: 978-1-58923-729-2

10 9 8 7 6 5 4 3 2 1

Library of Congress Cataloging-in-Publication Data available

Copy Editor: Peggy Wright
Proofreader: Karen Ruth
Book Design: Sandra Salamony
Photographs: Creative Publishing international and Glenn Scott Photography

Printed in China

PRECUT
PATCHWORK PARTY

MODERN PROJECTS
TO SEW AND CRAFT WITH
**FABRIC STRIPS, SQUARES,
AND FAT QUARTERS**

Elaine Schmidt

CONTENTS

THE BASICS

HOME DÉCOR PROJECTS

accessories, wearables, and gifts

INTRODUCTION

OK ... I have to admit it. I am a fabric addict! I love textiles of all types, from beautiful antique rugs and table linens to woven ribbons that look like mini tapestries to basic quilting cottons in every color of the rainbow. My stash of treasures is vast.

My car takes detours to fabric and quilting stores wherever I go, whether I am in my local area or any city I am visiting for business or pleasure. I have been known to arrive on vacation with a researched list of fabric stores in a given radius. I am never disappointed because something always inspires me for a new sewing or crafting project.

Now, more than ever, the array of colors and prints available in the fabric market is amazing. Manufacturers are working with incredibly talented artists to offer exciting collections of new designs every year.

I want them all, but let's face it, even if I won the lottery and had a huge fabric-buying budget, where would I put it? In satisfying my fabric addiction, I have discovered the joy of precut fabrics that allow me to purchase just a sampling of fabrics in a collection.

Although I have made some quilts, I also enjoy sewing and crafting projects to wear or display in my home or give as special gifts. Many patterns and books are available on creating beautiful quilts from precut fabrics. But how about using those bundles, strips, and squares for other projects? Because the manufacturers coordinate and precut the fabrics, they are the perfect head start to creating something wonderful.

I have designed the projects in this book to give you lots of ideas for using precut fabrics. The projects are not difficult to make; whether you are new to sewing or someone who has not sewn for a while, I hope you will enjoy making these projects your own. And just think ... now you'll have even more excuses for buying precut fabrics the next time you make a detour and stop at a fabric or quilting store.

THE BASICS

WHaT are PreCUT FaBrICS?

Precut fabrics are groups of coordinating fabrics that have been cut into specific sizes from yardage. They are themed by color, pattern, designer's collection, or fabric type. Typically, manufacturers make them from quilting-weight cotton fabrics. The number of pieces in each precut package varies, and often each group provides duplicates of designs.

Precut fabrics offer several advantages to sewers, quilters, and crafters. They are convenient to use and are always perfectly coordinated to offer a great assortment of print and color options that work together for any project. Precut fabrics save time as you can immediately get started on your project without the stress of selecting just the right coordinating fabrics.

Many people's least favorite activity when creating fabric projects is preparing and cutting the fabric. Precuts allow you to get started right away.

Precuts also save money since you do not have to purchase all the fabrics in a collection by the yard. In most stores, the smallest amount that staff will cut is ¼ yard (0.2 meter). If you had to purchase ¼-yard (0.2 meter) cuts of thirty different fabrics, the cost could really add up. Precuts also reduce waste as they often provide the exact sizes required for projects, with a minimal amount of trimming.

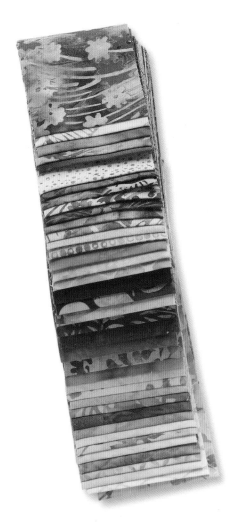

Fat Quarters

Most quilting-weight cotton fabrics are about 44" (111.8 cm) wide. A yard of fabric will measure 36" X 44" (91.4 X 111.8 cm). A quarter yard will measure 9" X 44" (22.9 X 111.8 cm), which is a long skinny size that is not always very useful. A fat quarter is also a quarter yard of fabric, but it is cut in a different way. To make a fat quarter, the fabric is first cut into a ½-yard (0.5 m) piece, measuring 18" X 44" (45.7 X 111.8 cm). Then it is cut again along the centerfold to make two fat quarters, each 18" X 22" (45.7 X 55.9 cm).

Stores sell fat quarters individually as well as in coordinating bundles wrapped together for a pretty presentation.

Using fat quarters versus quarter-yard cuts of fabric offers several advantages. Fat quarters are good for projects that require larger pieces of fabric; e.g., pillows, placemats and napkins. And fat quarters of larger-scale designs will include more of the entire printed pattern.

Fat Eighths

Fat eighths are half the size of fat quarters. They are cut to measure approximately 11" X 18" (27.9 X 45.7 cm) or 9" X 22" (22.9 X 55.9 cm). They are the same amount of fabric as an eighth of a yard that has been cut across the finished width. But like a fat quarter, they are a much more useful size. Fat eighths are also sold individually or in coordinated bundles. Fat eighths are not as commonly found in stores as fat quarters. Although I did not use this size of precuts in any of the projects in this book, you may find them useful for your own designs.

fat quarters

STrIPS

Precut strips are narrow cuts across the full width of the fabric, usually $2\frac{1}{2}$" X 44" (6.4 X 111.8 cm). Strips are generally sold in groups of 20, 30, or 40 pieces. Sometimes the collections will include duplicates of the fabric prints. Different manufacturers have different names for their precut strip collections. You will hear them referred to as designer rolls or jelly rolls or other clever names. Each roll should have a tag giving information about the fabrics, including the number of duplicates and the number of strips that the bundle includes.

Precut strips give you the most variety of colors and prints in a collection, and you can piece them together in many interesting ways.

strips

SQUareS

Precut fabric squares are typically 5" X 5" (12.7 X 12.7 cm) or 6" X 6" (15.2 X 15.2 cm). Manufacturers refer to the coordinating bundles as charm packs or charms. They get their name from traditionally made charm quilts that had no two fabrics with the same pattern. Like precut strips, manufacturers sell charm squares in packs of 20, 30, or 40 coordinating fabric squares. Check the label for the specifics.

Larger 10" X 10" (25.4 X 25.4 cm) squares are also available in precut bundles. Different manufacturers call them different names, and you will hear them referred to as layer cakes, stackers, or other clever names.

squares

SUPPLIES AND TOOLS

CUTTING TOOLS

When working with precut fabrics, you do not need to do as much cutting as you would when working with fabric yardage. Precuts give you a head start. I have designed the projects in this book to use the dimensions of the precuts and often the only cutting needed will be to cut strips to a given size or do a little trimming to even things up.

rotary cutters, cutting mats, and rulers

By far the cutting tool that I use the most when working with fabric is my rotary cutter. A rotary cutter resembles a pizza wheel. The handle houses a circular blade that is designed to make quick, straight cuts through several layers of fabric. The blade is extremely sharp. All rotary cutters have a safety lock, but you must still take care when handling the cutter. Follow the manufacturer's instructions for using the cutter and changing the blade. Rotary cutters come in many shapes and sizes. Look for one with an ergonomic handle that is comfortable for your hand.

To protect your work surface, you use a rotary cutter in conjunction with a rotary cutting mat. The mat has a surface that helps to hold the fabric flat and is made of a material that protects the rotary blade from becoming dull too quickly. Most rotary cutting mats are self-healing, which means that any cuts into the material will close up. Rotary cutting mats are available in several sizes. Most mats are printed with grids and ruler marks that help you to accurately cut fabrics straight and measured to the exact size you need for your project.

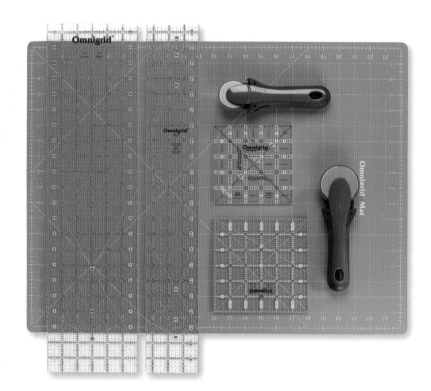

A wide variety of special rulers are available for use with your rotary cutter and mat. Manufacturers make them from a sturdy, clear plastic so you can see the pattern of the fabric you are cutting. They have easy-to-read horizontal and vertical measurements that allow you to accurately cut the fabric straight and at the desired length and width. Many different sizes and shapes of rulers are available. The ones I find most useful are 3" x 24" (7.6 x 61 cm), 6" x 24" (15.2 x 61 cm), and 6" x 12" (15.2 x 30.5 cm). Square rulers also come in handy for cutting squares and trimming blocks.

To trim precut strips to the length needed for a project, smooth the fabric on the mat, aligning one short edge with a marked line on the edge of the mat. Sometimes the selvage edges of a strip are a contrasting color or have printing on them, and you may want to trim them away. Place the long edge of the ruler along the long edge of the strip. Use the lines on the ruler to make sure the strip is straight on the cutting mat. Align the desired measurement line with the short edge of the strip. With your nondominant hand, hold the ruler down firmly with your finger tips, applying pressure and keeping your hand away from the edge of the ruler. Roll the rotary cutter away from you along the edge of the ruler to precisely trim away the excess fabric.

If you fold the strip, you will cut two pieces of the same length. If you place the fold of the strip on the edge of the mat and measure from the fold, you will cut a strip two times the length you've measured.

To use the rotary cutter and ruler to trim a fat quarter that might not be exactly straight and square, smooth the fabric on the mat and align the selvage edge with a straight-line mark on the side of the mat. Position the length of the ruler near one raw edge of the fabric. Use the markings on the ruler to perfectly align the ruler perpendicular to the selvage. Holding the ruler down firmly, roll the rotary cutter away from you along the long edge of the ruler to trim and straighten the fabric so the cut edge is at 90 degrees from the selvage edge.

Rotate the fabric and realign it with the marks on the mat. Trim the remaining two sides of the fat quarter so that the opposite sides are even and parallel.

scissors

Although I do not often use traditional sewing shears when working with precuts, I do like to have a good pair of small sharp scissors close at hand for trimming threads and seam allowances. Pinking shears that cut a sawtooth or zigzag edge are helpful for trimming raw fabric edges that may ravel.

CUTTING MACHINES

MANUAL FABRIC DIE-CUTTING MACHINES

Manual die-cutting machines that manufacturers have designed to work with fabric, such as the Sizzix Big Shot, make quick work of cutting shapes from precuts. With this type of machine, cutting out the shapes is done by applying downward pressure on the die blades. This causes the desired die shapes to be cut out in a stamping action. There are many different dies available, and they are wonderful for cutting fabric motifs to appliqué and also for creating your own precut strips and squares from fabrics you may have in your stash.

electronic fabric die cutting machines

Electronic fabric die cutters, such as the Slice Fabrique, use computer software to control their cutting blades. They come with design cards that contain several themed shapes and fonts for creating many different types of designs. Operating the machine is simple and involves inserting the design card, choosing the designs to be cut and then sizing the design for your particular project. There are also options for changing the cutting speed and blade pressure. Precut squares that have been backed with fusible web can be cut with electronic die cutters.

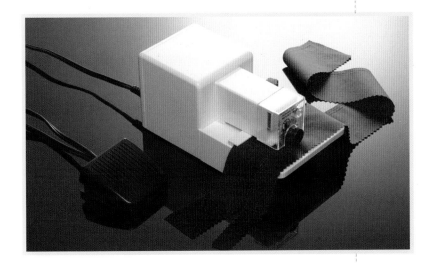

rotary cutting machines

If you want to cut strips from your stash of fabrics to make your own collection of 2½" (6.4 cm) precut strips to use for the projects in this book, a rotary cutting machine makes the job quick and easy on your hands. The machine has straight and pinked-edge rotary cutting blades and a foot pedal that allows you to guide the fabric through the machine to cut even fabric strips.

THReaDS aND NOTIONS

Sewing precuts together requires a lot of straight machine stitching and thread. Select a good quality thread that coordinates with the colors in the different precut prints. You do not have to use the same color thread throughout the project. In fact, I find that working with precuts is the perfect time to use up odds and ends of threads leftover from other projects. As long as the colors coordinate with the colors in the precut fabrics, go ahead and combine them. It's okay to use a different color of thread in the bobbin and the top. And every row of top-stitching does not have to be the same color. The different thread colors add to the mix of colors and patterns of the fabrics, giving a modern, improvisational look to your projects.

Other sewing notions you will need for the projects in this book are hand-sewing needles, sharp pins, a disappearing fabric marker, covered button kits, elastic, and bias tape. Some projects also use rickrack trims and ribbons. Beautiful ribbons that coordinate perfectly with the designer prints of various precut collections are now available on the market. Look for all these notions at your local craft, sewing, or quilting store.

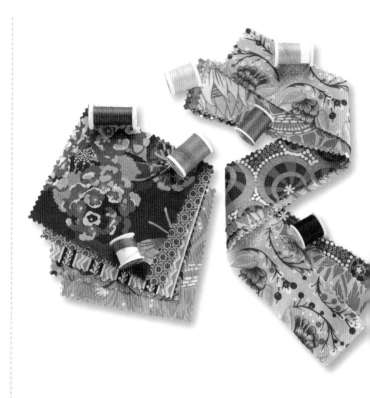

fLEECE, BATTING, INTERFACING, FUSIBLES, AND GLUES

Many of the precut fabric projects in this book instruct you to sew the fabric pieces to a fleece or batting backing. This backing adds a layer of softness and a little body. You can use either a cotton or polyester fleece or batting. Select one that is thin and that you can easily sew. For special projects, such as potholders, oven mitts, and table pads, look for insulated needle-punched fleece. This insulating liner is needle-punched through a reflective, metalized material and reflects hot or cold back to its source.

For some projects it is helpful to use a fusible fleece. This product eliminates the need to pin or sew basting stitches. The heat of your iron will activate the fusible adhesive and allow the fleece to adhere to the fabric. Fusible interfacings and stabilizers are also very useful to add body to projects. They vary in weight and crispness depending upon the thickness of the interfacing and the fabric to which it will be attached. Some are double-sided with the fusible surface on both sides. Check the manufacturers' labels for details on the types of uses for the specific products and how you should apply them. Paper-backed fusible web is good to have on hand when making appliqués. It makes any fabric into a fusible fabric. Fusible web is available by the yard as well as in rolls of narrow tape. The tapes are helpful for attaching trims and positioning narrow fabric strips in place. Follow the manufacturer's specific instructions on the best way to work with each fusible product.

I also recommend the use of quality fabric glue and a fabric-basting adhesive spray for some projects. Look for all of these products at your local craft, sewing, or quilting store.

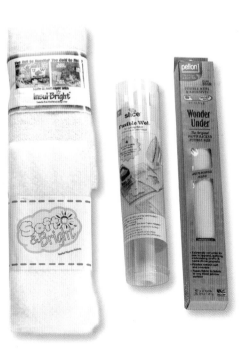

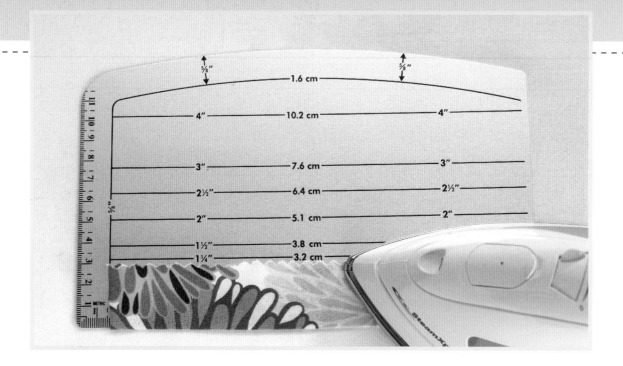

SEWING MACHINES AND IRONS

You don't need a fancy sewing machine to work with precuts and make the projects in this book. You may only occasionally want to do a zigzag stitch to overcast a raw edge and keep it from fraying or perhaps to make a buttonhole. Most of the time, you will only sew straight seams.

You do want to have a good steam iron and an ironing board for pressing fabrics, ironing seam allowances, and applying fusibles. It is important to press as you go. This practice will keep your project clean and neat. You may want to use spray sizing on the precuts to give them a little crispness and body. It is not as stiff as starch and is useful if you are making your own precut fabrics from yardage that you have already washed and dried.

One of the most used tools in my studio is a metal hem gauge for accurately pressing back the edges of fabric to a specific depth. You will not need to use a separate ruler if you have this gauge. Although it can get hot from the heat of the iron, the gauge protects your fingers when pressing back seam allowances and hems.

OTHER USEFUL TOOLS

Manufacturers are always developing new products to make sewing and crafting fun and a little easier to do. Below is a list of a few of my favorite new tools.

FASTURN™ TOOL

I've always loved using stitched fabric strips in my projects, but I hate turning the narrow tubes right side out. That dislike changed the day I discovered the Fasturn tool. It makes easy work of turning sewn tubes, no matter the length. I use the #5 size, a 1/2" (1.3 cm) diameter tube for quickly turning sewn 2½" (6.4 cm) precut strips right side out.

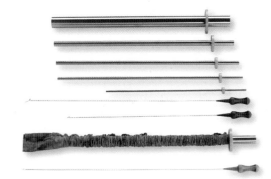

I-TOP™ BUTTON MAKER

Fabric-covered buttons are the perfect accent for many of the precut fabric projects I design. The i-top button maker is an ergonomically designed tool that easily creates covered buttons. The metal button forms, called Button Daddies, come in four sizes and quickly snap together with the tool. Small leftover bits of precut strips make great covered buttons.

BIAS TAPE MAKER MACHINE

Precut strips are cut across the width of the fabric, on the straight of grain. Although they are not cut on the bias, you can use them to bind the straight edges of a square or rectangular project, or you can fold and press them to use as a finished trim. The Bias Tape Maker Machine allows you to quickly fold and press strips into single- or double-fold tape at the touch of a button. You do not have to cut the strips on the bias to work with the machine. By not having to use a hot iron to fold back the raw edges of the fabric strip, you won't have to worry about burning your fingers or keeping the folds uniform and straight. This machine does it all for you. I use the 1¼" (3.2 cm) single-fold tip and the 1¼" (3.2 cm) quilt-binding tip with 2½" (6.4 cm) precut strips.

WORKING WITH PRECUT FABRICS

PREPARATION

Precut fabrics are ready to use in your projects. Check the label for any care instructions. Generally speaking, I do not prewash precut fabrics. Since all of the fabrics are coming from the same collection and are printed on the same type of base fabric, any shrinkage will be equal for all the fabrics when you wash them. If you are concerned about shrinkage or colors running when washed, you can hand wash the precuts, taking care not to over-handle them. Although the cut edges of some precuts may be pinked, they will begin to unravel when agitated. Do not wash precut fabrics in the washing machine and do not put them in the dryer.

To wash fat quarters, strips, and squares by hand, separate the pieces by similar colors. Fill a large sink with cold water. Add a mild detergent and swish the water around to get the soap evenly distributed. Place the precuts in the water and very gently swirl them until they are all wet. Let the fabrics soak for 15–20 minutes. Drain the soapy water and rinse the fabrics completely under cool running water. Make sure all the soap residue is out of the fabrics. Squeeze excess water out of fabrics with a thirsty towel and lay the pieces flat to air dry a bit. Press the pieces while still damp and lightly spray with sizing to restore crispness, if desired.

Once you have completed your project and have properly finished or hidden the seam allowances, you can wash and dry the fabrics as the manufacturer instructs.

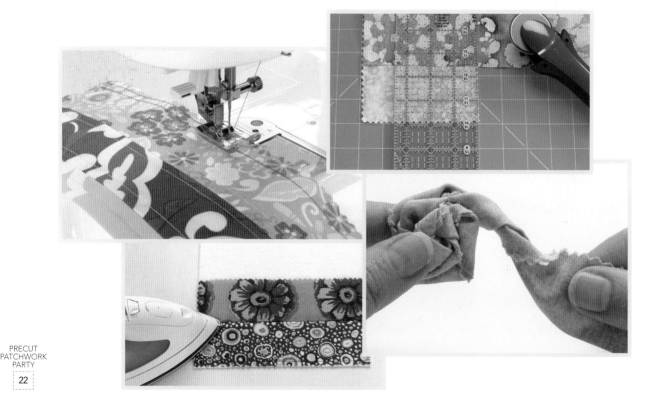

Sewing with Precut Fabrics

Once you unroll a package of precut strips, unfold a bundle of fat quarters, or open a package of charm squares, the magic starts to happen. Look through the different fabric designs. You may want to pull out your favorites or any that you feel are accent prints. You can separate lights and darks to help you create a project that showcases the differences in the various coordinating patterns.

Stitching the pieces together is simple. Put the selected precuts right sides together and sew them with straight machine stitches. For most of the projects in this book, I have pieced the precuts together with a seam allowance of $\frac{1}{4}$" (6 mm) or $\frac{1}{2}$" (1.3 cm). If the edges of the pieces are pinked with a zigzag edge, place the outermost tips of the zigzags along the desired marking on your sewing-machine's guides. To assure that pieces will line up and be the correct size, make sure to be consistent in sewing the seams together so the seam allowances are the same width throughout the project.

I usually do not find it necessary to pin before I stitch. If I have to adjust the edges of the precuts that I am sewing together, I stop stitching with the needle in the down position, align the edges of the precuts, and then continue stitching the seam. When sewing two patched rows together, however, I do use pins to match seams so they will align when sewn. It is a good idea to add pins to the seam allowances so they lie flat when sewn.

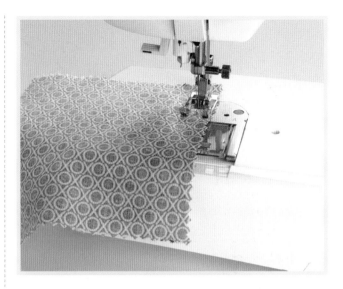

IRONING AND FINISHING SEAMS

One of the most important things to remember when working with precut fabrics is ironing seams flat before progressing to the next step in your project's construction. Since the vast majority of precut fabrics are 100% cotton, use a hot iron with steam.

You can either press seams to one side or press them open. Press from both the front and back of the fabric and make sure that the pressed seams are completely flat in each step.

If the seams in the project are hidden or if you will not launder the project, it is not necessary to finish the seams. Some precut strips and charm squares have pinked edges that will help to keep the fabric from fraying. Other precuts do not have this zigzag edge and if you are using them for projects that you will launder, such as aprons or skirts, it is a good idea to finish the seams. You can trim the raw edges of the precuts with pinking shears or can finish them with topstitching.

TOPSTITCHED SEAMS

Topstitching is straight machine stitching, typically sewn from the right side of the fabric. Not only does the topstitching hold the seams flat, but also it keeps the raw edges from unraveling when agitated in the washer and dryer. When you press the seams to one side, topstitch them with one row of stitching through the seam allowance, close to the seam. When you press the seams open, topstitch them on each side, close to each side of the seam line. If the seam allowances are $\frac{1}{4}$" (6 mm) wide, topstitch them $\frac{1}{8}$" (3 mm) from the seam line. If the seam allowances are $\frac{1}{2}$" (1.3 cm) wide, topstitch them $\frac{1}{4}$" (6 mm) from the seam line.

FreNcH seaMs

Sometimes you do not want the raw edges of a seam allowance to be exposed, especially if the project gets lots of wear or might have to stand up to repeated laundering or if the wrong side of the fabric may show, such as with a curtain panel. For a neat finish, it is best to use a French seam. A French seam looks like a plain seam from the right side and a narrow tuck on the wrong side.

To sew a French seam:

1   Place the fabric wrong sides together.

2   Stitch ⅛" (3 mm) from the raw edges.

3   Press the seam allowance to one side.

4   Fold and press the fabric right sides together, keeping the stitching line at the center of the fold.

5   Stitch ¼" (6 mm) away from the first line of stitching. The raw edges will be encased inside the tuck. Check to make sure you have no raveled threads that are showing.

6   Press the seam to one side.

French seams are difficult to sew in curved areas, but they are perfect for finishing the many straight seams you encounter when working with precut fabrics.

[2]

[4]

[5]

MAKING YOUR OWN PRECUTS

Precuts are so easy and tempting to buy, but you may find you can create your own collections of precuts from your stash of fabrics. Cutting remnants and small yardage pieces into strips, squares, and fat quarters may inspire you, help you to coordinate your leftover fabrics, and get started on any of the projects in this book. You'll want to select at least ten fabrics that work well together.

SELECTING FABRICS FROM YOUR STASH

Perhaps you have purchased a few fabrics from one designer's collection. That set of fabrics could be the start of a set of precuts. To those fabrics, you can add small prints, such as dots, squiggles, and checks that coordinate with the colors in the designer's fabrics. You can also add solid fabrics. Look carefully at all the colors in the designer's patterns and pull out fabrics that are a similar tone. You might be surprised to see how good they look together.

   If you find that you love a particular color and have many fabrics in that color range, pull them together to make precuts. I love green so I always seem to have a large range of green fabrics, from bright yellow green to dark hunter green. When you group them together, they can work very nicely in a project.

You might also want to make a group of pre-cuts all from one type of fabric, such as checks or dots. Think about another type of pattern that would work well with those patterns, perhaps stripes to continue the graphic look.

CUTTING PRECUT SHAPES

Use a rotary cutter, mat, and rulers to cut your stash pieces into standard precut sizes. You can cut fat quarters from larger pieces of fabric. Cut an 18" (45.7 cm) length across the width of the fabric and then cut it cut it in half at the fold parallel to the selvage. Use a ruler to quickly cut 2½" (6.4 cm) strips across the width of the fabric. Make sure that the beginning cut edge is straight and perpendicular to the selvage edge. Square rulers make it easy to cut charm squares. Die-cutting machines have dies available for cutting several strips and squares at one time.

General Techniques

Binding Edges with Precut Strips

You can use 2½" (6.4 cm) precut strips to finish the edges of many projects. Precut strips are cut on the straight crosswise grain of the fabric. Traditionally binding fabrics are cut on the bias, which allows them to stretch a bit and smoothly cover curved edges. But straight-grain bindings work just fine for binding the raw edges of projects that do not curve. You can easily finish anything with a straight edge with a precut strip binding, such as quilts, placemats, garments, etc.

Since precut strips are only 43"–44" (109.2–111.8 cm) wide, you may need to piece several strips together to make a length long enough to sew around all edges of your project. Sew the strips together with a ¼" (6 mm) seam allowance and press the seams open. You can sew together strips of the same fabric print, but it is also fun to sew together various lengths of strips in different coordinating prints to make a patchwork binding.

Sewing the Binding to the Project

1   Sew together strips to create enough binding to go around your project plus a few inches for turning corners and overlapping the ends.

2   Press back the beginning end ¼" (6 mm) and iron the binding strip in half.

3   Place the doubled binding strip onto the right side of the project, aligning the raw edges. Starting 2" (5 cm) from the turned-back end, stitch the binding to the project with a ¼" (6 mm) seam allowance. Stop the stitches ¼" (6 mm) from the corner's edge. Back stitch and cut the threads.

4   Fold the binding up, making a 45-degree angle.

5   Keeping the diagonal fold in place, fold the binding back down and align the raw edge with the edge of the next side of the project.

6   Starting at the point where the last stitching ended, stitch down the next side.

7   Continue to sew the binding around all the edges in this way. When you reach the beginning, trim the binding so that you can tuck about ½" (1.3 cm) of the end into the beginning end. Continue to stitch across the overlap, lining up with the beginning stitches.

8   Turn the binding to the back. Align the folded edge with the stitching line and hand stitch in place, folding a miter at each corner.

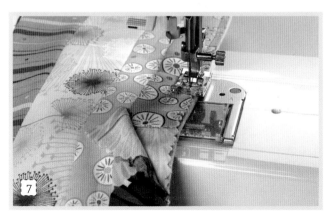

STITCH AND FLIP QUILTING

This quilt-as-you-go technique is great to use with precut fabric strips and squares. It allows you to sew pieces together and quilt them to a batting or background fabric at the same time.

Begin by selecting the background onto which you want to quilt the pieces. In most of the projects in this book, I have quilted the precuts onto thin fleece or batting or fusible fleece that I have ironed onto a background fabric.

1 With the right side up, place the first precut piece of fabric along the outer edge of the batting or backing fabric and stitch close to the outer edge.

2 Place the second piece on top of the first, right sides together. Stitch them together ¼" (6 mm) from the raw edge. The stitches will also secure the pieces to the batting or backing fabric.

3 Flip the second piece back so that it is right side up. Press it flat.

4 Continue to sew on pieces one at a time, flipping and ironing each piece as you sew it.

5 From time to time, use a clear ruler to make sure that the stitched rows are parallel to the beginning edge. If necessary, make small adjustments to the stitching lines to keep them even and straight. Small adjustments will not be noticeable in the finished project, but it is important to continue to check the measurements before the rows become too much out of alignment.

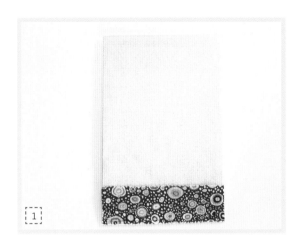

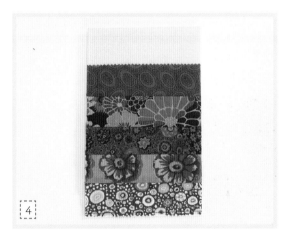

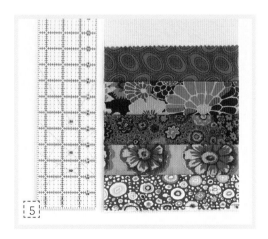

THE
BASICS

LOG CABIN PATCHWORK

Some traditional patchwork patterns, such as the log cabin block, are super quick to sew together with precuts. This patchwork block starts with a center square. You then position surrounding rows or strips around the square. Patchwork blocks are not just for making quilts. They make beautiful pillows or tablecloths, or you can use them as the accent for a handbag or almost any project you want to create.

1   Select a square for the center of the block. In my sample, I used a 5" (12.7 cm) square. Depending upon the size you'd like the finished block to be, you could use a 6" (15.2 cm) or 10" (25.4 cm) precut charm square.

2   With the right sides together, place a 2½" (6.4 cm) strip across the top of the square and stitch. Depending upon the desired size of the finished block, the seam allowance can be ¼" (6 mm) or ½"(1.3 cm). Trim the excess fabric straight with the edge of the square.

3   Press the seam allowance toward the strip.

4   In the same way, sew a strip to the right side of the square. Trim excess fabric and press the seam allowance.

5   In the same way, continue to add strips to the bottom and left side of the center square.

6   Add as many rows of strips around the center square until the block is the size you need. Colors can alternate in each row to create a repeating pattern or you can select strips randomly for a more varied effect.

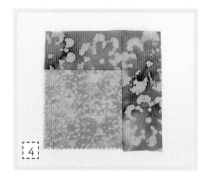

appliqué

Appliqué means to "place upon." Fabric appliqués are cut-out decorations attached to a background fabric. Traditionally, you cut out shapes, turn back the raw edges, and handstitch the designs to the background. Now with the use of paper-backed fusible web, you can quickly fuse the appliqués in place with an iron and then machine- or handstitch them to decoratively finish the edges.

Following the manufacturer's instructions, iron fusible web to the back of a precut square or left-over bit of any precut piece. When it's cool, draw or trace a design onto the paper backing and cut it out. Note that if the design is one-way, such as an alphabet letter, you need to draw the reverse image of the design so that the right side of the fabric will be face up to appliqué in place.

The easiest way to make an appliqué design is to use one of the many shapes available on a manual or electronic fabric die-cutting machine. This technique requires no drawing, and the cutting is quick and accurate.

Remove the paper from the back of the appliqué and iron the shape to your project. If you will launder the project or it will be subject to wear, finish the edges with hand or machine stitches, such as straight, blanket, or satin stitch.

With a little planning, you can efficiently use every scrap of a precut square. The advantage of using a cutting machine is that you do not have to cut into the fabric to cut out the shape. The blade of the cutter just cuts the line around the design, leaving you with the design and the reverse image cut from the fabric. You can use both pieces in a project. To do so, make sure to center the appliqué design in the square on the cutting machine. You can appliqué both the positive and negative image to your project.

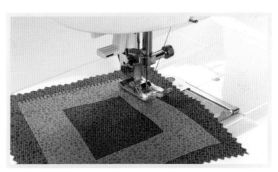

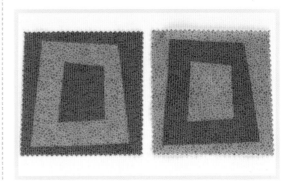

FaBrIC TrIMS

Precut fabric strips give you a head start for making a wide variety of fabric trims and embellishments.

STITCHeD anD TurneD STrIPS

When you stitch precut fabric strips together and turn them right side out, you create a fabric tube that you can use in many different ways. Because these stitched and turned strips have no raw edges that will fray and unravel, you can use them like a ribbon, everything from tying a bow to making a trim.

The tricky part of making finished strips is turning them right side out after you have sewn them, especially if the strip is long. The following technique can make that job a little easier.

1 Cut a length of scrap ribbon or cord the length of the fabric strip plus 3" (76 mm).

2 Lay the ribbon or cord on the right side of the fabric strip. Leave about ½" (1.3 cm) of the ribbon or cord above the end of the strip.

3 Fold the strip with the right sides together, lining up the raw edges.

4 Sew across the end of the strip, catching the ribbon or cord in the stitching. Backstitch the end to secure the stitching. Continue sewing down the side of the entire length of the strip. Do not catch the ribbon or cord in the side seam. Sew a ¼" (6 mm) seam for a 1" (2.5 cm) finished strip.

5 With one hand, gently pull on the ribbon or cord. With the other hand, ease the fabric along as it gathers up. At the stitched end, encourage the fabric to turn itself inside the tube.

6 Continuing to pull on the ribbon or cord, slowly pull the entire strip through until it is right side out.

7 Cut off the end of the ribbon or cord.

8 With slightly dampened fingers, roll the seam to one side and iron the finished strip flat.

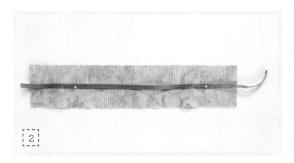

2

5

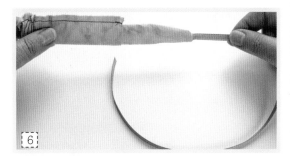

6

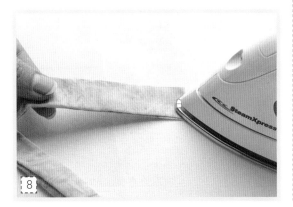

8

The Fasturn tool makes it very quick and easy to turn fabric strips, especially long lengths. You don't have to sew a ribbon or cord into the strip. Following the manufacturer's instructions, sew the edges of the strip together, place it over the ½" (1.3 cm) cylinder tube, and turn it right side out with the wire hook.

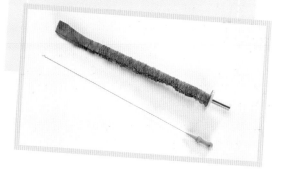

Fabric rickrack

You can gather stitched and turned strips along a zigzag line to form a scalloped trim that looks like jumbo rickrack. It's a perfect custom trim for precut fabric projects.

1 Start with a stitched and turned fabric strip approximately 3 times the length of the finished trim you want to make.

2 With a disappearing marker, place a mark every 3" (7.6 cm) along one edge of the strip. On the other edge, begin the marks 1½" (3.8 cm) from the end and continue to place marks every 3" (7.6 cm).

3 Thread a needle with double thread and knot it. Sew long handstitches from one mark across the center of the strip to the next mark, zigzag style.

4 Pull up the stitches and evenly gather the strip as you sew along the length. Secure the pulled-up stitches every few inches with a few backstitches.

5 Press the gathered trim flat, forming an even scalloped edge on both sides of the strip.

6 Sew the finished rickrack to your project with hand or machine stitches down the center of the trim.

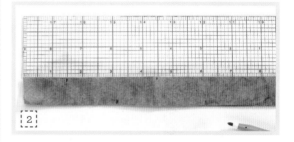

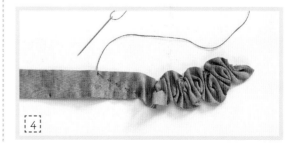

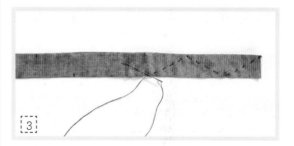

3 Pull up the stitches to gather the circles and place the pom-pom inside the circle. Tighten the stitches and use the tip of a pencil or the pointed end of a pair of small scissors to make sure all of the pom-pom is tucked inside the circle. Knot the thread securely to hold it.

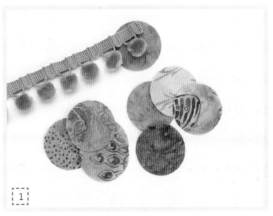

FabriC covered Pom-Poms

I have always loved pom-pom trim because it adds a special touch of whimsy, but the available colors are very limited. Covering the pom-poms on purchased trim with fabric circles makes a trim that not only coordinates perfectly with your project but also adds even more fun, especially when you randomly cover each of the pom-poms in different prints.

1 Gather up leftover bits of precut fabric strips. To determine the size of the fabric circle you will need to cut to cover the pom-poms, measure the diameter of the individual pom-poms on the purchased trim. Multiply that measurement by 2 and add 1" (2.5 cm). That measurement will be the diameter of the circles that you will need to cut. The pom-poms on the trim shown in the photo measure $\frac{1}{2}$" (1.3 cm) in diameter. I cut my circles to be 2" (5 cm) in diameter. A fabric die cutter makes quick work of accurately cutting the circles.

2 Thread a needle with double thread and knot it. Finger-press the fabric edge back a scant $\frac{1}{4}$" (6 mm) as you sew long gathering stitches around the circle.

PLeaTS

You can fold precut strips and pleat them to make custom decorative accent trims. You can sew the pleated strips along one side and insert the raw edges into a seam, such as around a pillow. Because pleated trims are fairly flexible, you can use them around gentle curves and corners. You also can stitch the pleated fabric strips down the center and then sew them to a project.

Depending upon the depth of the pleats, you will need fabric strips at least three times the desired finished length of the trim. It is a good idea to do a small sample of the pleating size to see exactly how much yardage of the strips you will need. You can sew precut strips in various lengths together, and they do not all have to be the same fabric print or color. Because fabrics within a roll of precut strips coordinate, pieced strips will work together to make a fun accent to your project.

KNIFe PLeaTS

You fold knife pleats with all the pleats going in the same direction.

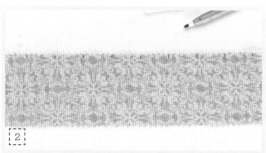

1 For a doubled-fabric pleated trim with a fold at the lower edge, fold the 2½" (6.4 cm) strip in half, wrong sides together. For a single layer trim with a finished edge, sew a narrow hem on one long side of the strip. Or if the raw edge of the strip is pinked with a zigzag edge and you will not wash the trim, you can leave it unfinished or simply finish it with a line of straight stitching ¼" (6 mm) from the outside edge.

2 Using an air-soluble fabric marker, place marks along the top edge of the fabric strip. Place the marks the distance apart for the desired depth of the pleats; for example, for 1" (2.5 cm) pleats, place the marks 1" (2.5 cm) apart.

3 Starting with the third mark from the end of the strip, fold the fabric up to the first mark and pin it. Continue to pleat the fabric in the same

[4]

easy PLeaTing

- After you have sewn a few pleated strips, you may find that you do not need to pin each pleat before sewing it in place. With your machine needle stopped in the down position, stitch across the first fold, fold the next pleat in place and continue stitching. Continue to fold and stitch the length of the strip.

- To eliminate the need to mark the folds, use Perfect Pleating Tape. Follow the manufacturer's instructions to apply the tape along the length of the strip. Pleat using the guidelines on the tape. Stitch and remove the tape. Super easy!

way the entire length of the strip. The third mark from the fold is always brought up to the first visible mark after the previous pleat.

4   Sew the folded pleats in place close to the raw edge of the strip.

5   You can press the pleats flat for a crisp look or leave them unironed for a softer pleat.

BOX PLeaTs

You fold box pleats with the under edges toward the center of each pleat, creating a box shape on the front of the trim.

1   Prepare and mark the fabric strips as instructed for knife pleats, Steps 1–2.

2   Starting with the third mark from the end of the strip, fold the fabric up to the first mark and pin it.

3   Bring the third mark from the folded pleat up the back of the strip to the first mark on the fabric and pin it. This action creates the first box.

4   Bring the second mark from the folded edge of the first pleat up to the last folded edge of the first pleat and pin it.

5   Bring the third mark from the last fold up the back of the strip to the first mark and pin it. This action creates the second box. Continue in this same way to make box pleats the entire length of the strip.

6   Sew the folded pleats in place close to the raw edge of the strip. Press the pleats or leave them unironed.

[3]

[5]

Flowers and Leaves

You can make flowers from fabric in many ways. I like to use precut strips or squares so I have less fabric cutting before getting started and can get right to the fun part. Fabric flowers make wonderful embellishments for all types of projects, from home décor to wearables. The following is a list of a few of my favorite fabric flowers. Why not make several pairs and sew or glue them to shoe-clip findings and attach them to a pair of ballet flats; make every outfit special.

Gathered rosette

1 Cut a 10"–16" (25.4–40.6 cm) fabric strip, depending on how full you'd like the rosette to be.

2 Form a ring by sewing the short ends together with a ¼" (6 mm) seam allowance. Press the seam open.

3 Fold the fabric in half, wrong sides together, and press it. With thread doubled in the needle, sew a line of long gathering stitches near the raw edges.

4 Pull up the stitches to gather the ring tightly to form the rosette shape. Secure the stitches to hold the gathers.

5 Sew a button to the center of the rosette.

2

3

4

You also can sew the gathering stitches along the folded edge of the fabric ring. This action will make the raw edges of the fabric the outer edges of the rosette. After you have gathered the rosette, separate the two layers for a full rosette. Many precut strips have pinked edges that will not fray very much, but even if the fabric strip has a straight-cut edge, slightly unraveled edges look fine and natural. You can clip away any long threads.

To make a larger layered rosette, cut a 16"–20" (40.6–50.8 cm) fabric strip and stitch it into a ring. Finish one edge with a narrow hem. Gather the single layer of fabric with long stitches along the unfinished edge. Sew a gathered rosette as described above onto the center of the larger layer.

raggedy rosette

1 Cut a 12"–18" (30.5–45.7 cm) fabric strip, depending upon how full you'd like the rosette to be.

2 Fold the strip in half, wrong sides together and sew a line of long gathering stitches near the raw edges.

3 Using sharp scissors, cut into the fabric, from the folded edge toward the stitching line. Do not cut through the stitching. Make the cuts ¼"–½" (6 mm–1.3 cm) apart. It is fine if they vary in distance. Do not worry about cutting very precisely. The more random the cuts, the more natural the look of the finished rosette will be.

4 Pull up the stitches to gather the rosette and knot the thread securely to hold it.

5 Add a button to the center of the rosette. If using sew-through buttons, sew a smaller button on top of a larger button for an additional colorful detail.

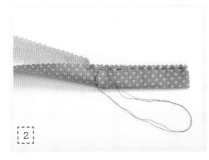

2

3

4

folded rosette

1 For each folded rosette, you will need a 14" (35.6 cm) stitched and turned strip. Hold the strip with the seam at the bottom. Fold the strip at a 60 degree angle at the center and press the strip.

2 Bring the strip from the right side over the left, folding it to align with the side of the first fold. Press and pin the folds.

3 Rotate the point created to the left a little and bring the strip that is hanging on the right over to the left. Make sure to fold it against the inside edge of the left side strip. Press and pin the folds.

4 In the same way, rotate the points and bring the strip that is hanging on the right over to the left. Press and pin the folds.

5 Again, rotate the points and bring the strip hanging on the right over to the left. To assure that the rosette is symmetrical, the edge of strip at this turn should be parallel to the edge of the first fold. Press and pin the folds.

6 Repeat this folding pattern to make the 5th side of the rosette. Press and pin the folds.

7 In the same way, fold the 6th and final side of the rosette. Slip the tails of the strips under the first point. Press and pin the folds.

8 Trim the excess fabric and handstitch the layers to hold them securely.

9 Because no raw edges show from the front, it is not necessary to sew a button to the center of this rosette, but you can add it, if desired.

1

2

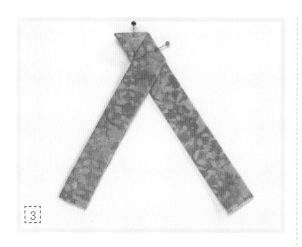

[3]

[4]

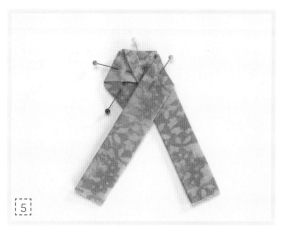

[5]

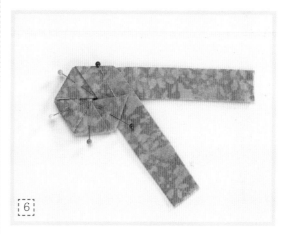

[6]

[7]

[8]

rolled rosette

You can use rolled rosettes alone or add them to the center of a gathered rosette.

1 Use a 22" (55.9 cm) fabric strip to make a rolled rosette 2" (5 cm) in diameter. Fold the strip in half and press it, wrong sides together. Tie an overhand knot close to one end of the strip.

2 Hold the knot in your nondominant hand. This knot will be the center of the rolled rosette. Twist the folded strip and wrap it around the center knot. Secure the strip with fabric glue as you twist and wrap the strip around the center knot.

3 The rose will grow larger as you wrap and twist the entire strip around the center knot. When you reach the other end of the strip, fold and glue it to the back of the rosette. If desired, glue a circle of felt to the back of the rosette.

4 Alternatively, you can form the rolled rosette on a circle of double-sided adhesive. This method is a good way to make a rolled rosette for a project that you will not launder. Cut a 2" (5 cm) circle of adhesive and remove the paper backing from one side. Place the knot at the center of the circle. Wrap and twist the fabric around the knot and push it onto the adhesive to hold. Remove the remaining paper backing from the back of the rosette. Stick the end of the fabric strip to the back and position the rosette onto your project.

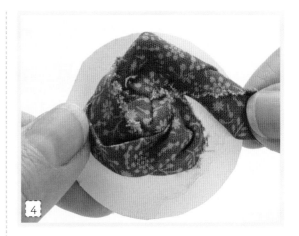

Fabric Leaves

You can make fabric leaves from stitched and turned strips (page 34). Use a 5"–6" (12.7–15.2 cm) finished strip for a single leaf. Overlap the ends to form a loop and pin. To make a set of double leaves, use a 10"–12" (25.4–30.5 cm) strip. Overlap the end to form a loop and then form the strip into a figure 8, forming two loops. You can sew leaves with hand stitches or glue them to the back of any fabric flower.

For raggedy leaves, fold the strips in half, leaving the raw edges exposed. Overlap as described above to form the leaves.

HOME DÉCOR PROJECTS

reversible
table runner

You sew this reversible table runner from precut fabric strips. You construct one side from vertical rows of fabric strips and the other side from horizontal rows. The approximate finished size is 14" × 42" (35.6 × 106.7 cm).

YOU WILL NEED

PRECUT FABRICS

- eighteen 2½" (6.4 cm) strips: 7 for the side with the vertical rows, 8 for the side with the horizontal rows, and 3 for the binding.

OTHER SUPPLIES AND TOOLS

- a 14" x 42" (35.6 x 106.7 cm) rectangle of fusible fleece
- coordinating sewing thread
- sewing machine and iron
- usual sewing supplies

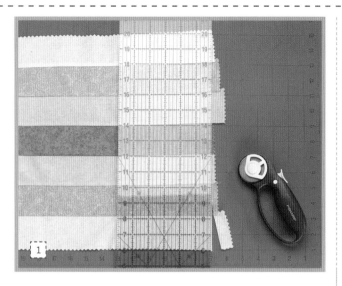

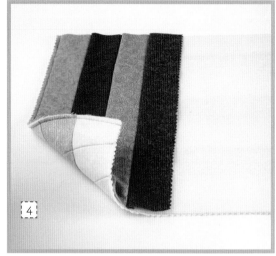

PUTTING IT TOGETHER

1 Place the seven strips you have selected for the vertical side of the runner in a pleasing color arrangement. With the right sides together, sew the strips to each other along the long edges, using a ¼" (6 mm) seam allowance. Press seams to one side. Use a rotary cutter and ruler to trim the ends of the strips so that all the rows are even and straight.

2 Following manufacturer's instructions, fuse the fleece to the back of the vertically pieced side of the runner.

3 Cut twenty-three 14" (356 mm) strips from the precuts you have selected for the horizontal side of the runner. Arrange the cut strips in a repeating pattern or random order.

4 Following the stitch-and-flip quilting technique (page 30), sew the horizontal strips one at a time to the fleece side of the runner. Flip and press each strip as it is sewn. Use a ruler to check from time to time to make sure that you are sewing the rows straight.

5 If necessary, trim the end of the vertical side to align with the edge of the last stitched horizontal row.

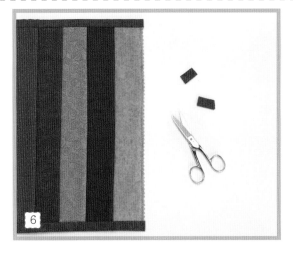

Make it yours

- Look for contrasting colors and patterns in the precut rolls of fabric strips. If you want a different look for each side of the runner, use light colors for one side and dark colors for the opposite side.

- You can make the runner any length or width. Piece fabric strips together and cut them to the desired finished length of the runner. Sew them together in a random pattern for the vertical side of the runner. Cut the horizontal rows to fit the desired width of the pieced vertical side.

- The runner does not need to be reversible. Use a rectangle of plain muslin or any coordinating print for the back.

- You can use the same technique to make placemats.

6 Use two strips to bind the long sides of the runner. Press and sew them (page 28). Trim the ends even with the short sides of the runner.

7 Cut two 15½" (39.4 cm) strips for the remaining binding sections. Press and sew them to the short sides of the runner, folding in excess fabric before slip-stitching the edges.

MIX & MATCH
PLACEMATS, NAPKINS, AND NAPKIN RINGS

One roll of precut strips and twelve fat quarters will create a set of four placemats, reversible lined napkins, and coordinating napkin rings. Mix and match the patterns to make each mat a little different in the placement of the patterns. Select two different prints for each napkin and use the leftover strips to make the rosette napkin rings.

YOU WILL NEED

PRECUT FABRICS FOR 4 PLACEMAT SETS

- one roll of 2½" (6.4 cm) strips; you need a minimum of 24 strips, but it's fun to have a few more to mix and match.
- 12 coordinating fat quarters

OTHER SUPPLIES AND TOOLS

- ⅞ yard (.8 m) of 45" (114.3 cm) fusible fleece
- four 1" (2.5 cm) buttons to cover
- fabric marking pen
- coordinating sewing thread
- sewing machine and iron
- usual sewing supplies

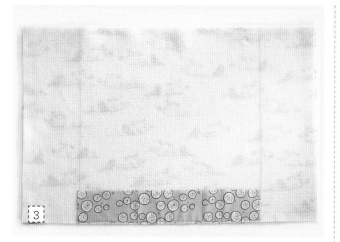

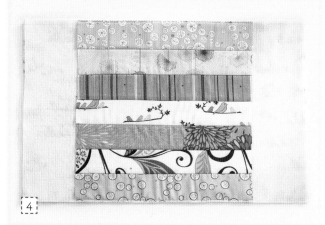

PUTTING IT TOGETHER

Use ¼" (6 mm) seam allowances throughout the construction.

PLACEMATS

1 For each mat, cut a 14" × 21" (35.6 × 53.3 cm) rectangle of fusible fleece. For the backing, cut a 14" × 21" (35.6 × 53.3 cm) rectangle from one fat quarter. Following the manufacturer's instructions, fuse the fleece to the wrong side of the backing fabric.

2 Cut seven 13" (33 cm) strips of different fabrics for the center of each mat. Cut four different 14" (35.6 cm) strips for the sides.

3 To place the center strips, draw two placement lines on the fleece, each 4" (10.2 cm) in from the short sides. Position the first strip onto the center bottom of the fleece and stitch close to the edge.

4 Following the stitch-and-flip quilting technique (page 30), sew the remaining six center strips to the center of the mat. Sew the edge of the last strip to the fleece. If necessary, trim excess fleece and backing along the edge of the last strip.

5 Place the edge of one side strip on each of the placement lines, making sure that they cover all the raw edges of the center strips.

6 Stitch and flip two strips to each side of the mat. If necessary, trim strips to fit the fleece and backing.

7 Sew the edge of the end strips to the fleece. If necessary, trim excess fleece and backing.

8 For the binding, stitch together a variety of leftover strips in various lengths to create a strip about 75" (190.5 cm) long. Following the binding instructions (page 28), bind all sides of the mat.

Napkins

1 Select two coordinating fat quarters for each napkin. Cut a 17½" (44.5 cm) square from both fabrics.

2 Place squares right sides together and stitch along all sides, leaving an opening along one side for turning.

3 Clip any excess fabric at corners and turn the napkins right side out. Press the napkins, making sure to evenly iron back seam allowance at the opening. Edge-stitch close to all sides of the finished napkin.

Napkin Rings

1 For the base of each napkin ring, cut two strips 7" (17.8 cm) long. Cut a length of fusible fleece 2½" × 7" (6.4 × 17.8 cm). Fuse the fleece to the wrong side on one strip.

2 With the right sides together, sew the two fabric strips together along all sides, leaving an opening for turning.

3 Clip any excess fabric at the corners and turn the piece right side out. Press it. Slipstitch the opening closed.

4

Make it Yours

- You can cut the back of the placemats from muslin or any fabric from your stash as it will not show from the front.

- You can make the placemats from all-horizontal or all-vertical strips.

- You can sew any number of side strips to the mat. You can sew the side strips only to one side for an asymmetrical look. Adjust the width of the center strips accordingly.

- To make the napkins unlined, use one fabric square and finish all sides with a machine-stitched, narrow, double hem.

- You can eliminate the gathered rosette from the napkin ring, or you can sew on a large button as an embellishment.

- Make extra napkins to coordinate with your mats so you'll have lots of mix-and-match options for several meals.

4 Slipstitch the short ends together to form a ring.

5 Following the gathered rosette instructions (page 40), cut a 12" (30.5 cm) strip and form it into a rosette. Cover a button with a contrasting, coordinating fabric and sew the button to the center of the rosette. Sew the finished rosette to the napkin ring at the center of the seam.

Patchwork
Table Topper

I have sewn together the all-shades-of-blue table topper with a center patchwork of charm squares and borders of precut strips.

The approximate finished size is 39" (99 cm) square.

YOU WILL NEED

PRECUT FABRICS
- twenty-five 6" (15.2 cm) charm squares
- twenty 2½" (6.4 cm) strips

OTHER SUPPLIES AND TOOLS
- coordinating sewing thread
- sewing machine and iron
- usual sewing supplies

3

5

PUTTING IT TOGETHER

Use ½" (1.3 cm) seam allowances throughout the construction of the table topper.

1 Arrange the charm squares five squares across and five rows down on your work table. Alternate light and dark colors and prints to create an interesting patchwork for the center of the table topper.

2 Sew five squares together to create each row of patchwork. Press all seams open and topstitch ¼" (6 mm) from each seam.

3 Sew five rows together to create the center of the table topper. Press all seams open and topstitch ¼" (6 mm) from each seam.

4 Sew a fabric strip to each side of the patchwork center. Trim excess fabric from strips. Press seams open and topstitch.

5 Sew a fabric strip to the top and bottom of the patchwork center. Trim excess fabric from strips. Press seams open and topstitch them.

7

make it yours

- To create a larger table topper, use more squares for the center section. To keep it square, use the same number of squares across and down, a total of 36 squares or 49 squares, etc.

- For a larger topper, you can use 10" (25.4 cm) charm squares for the center section.

- To make a tablecloth for a larger rectangular table, make the center section a rectangle. Use 6" (15.2 cm) or 10" (25.4 cm) charm squares.

- You can piece together fabric strips so that they are long enough to fit the size of a larger center section. Sew the strips together at the ends. Press the seams open and topstitch them. Use the sewn strips randomly to create a patchwork border around the center section.

- Use as many sewn border strips as needed to create a tablecloth for your desired finished dimensions.

6 Continue to add rows of fabric strips to the sides and then to the top and bottom edges of the center section. You add a total of 5 rows of strips around the center. As you add each strip, press the seams open and topstitch them.

7 Finish all sides of the table topper with a ½" (1.3 cm) double hem.

Director's chair cover

Sew precut strips to a heavy canvas base to make this director's chair cover. The instructions are for a chair cover that will fit a standard-sized director's chair sold in major import stores.

YOU WILL NEED

PRECUT FABRICS
- fourteen 2½" (6.4 cm) strips

OTHER SUPPLIES AND TOOLS
- ⅝ yard (.6 m) of 59" (149.7 cm)-wide heavy canvas fabric in a color that coordinates with the precut strips
- two ⅝" (16 mm) wooden sticks, 15" (38.1 cm) long (usually furnished with chair frame)
- coordinating sewing thread
- sewing machine and iron
- heavy-duty sewing machine needle
- usual sewing supplies

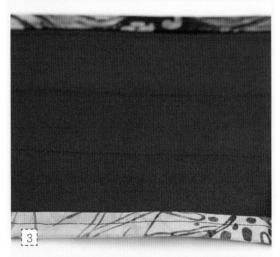

PUTTING IT TOGETHEr

Use a heavy duty sewing machine needle for this project as the canvas fabric is very thick.

1   For the chair back, cut a piece of canvas 10½" × 28" (26.7 × 71.1 cm). Cut 5 precut strips 28" (71.1 cm) long.

2   Arrange the strips in an interesting order and sew them to the canvas following the stitch-and-flip quilting technique (page 30). Evenly trim the canvas along both long sides to make the rectangle a finished width of 9½" (24.1 cm).

3   Fold back the long sides of the rectangle 1" (2.5 cm) and press them. Press the raw edges under to meet the crease and make a ½" (1.3 cm) double hem across the top and bottom of the chair back. Stitch close to the turned back edge.

4   Fold back the short sides of the rectangle 3½" (8.9 cm) and press them. Turn and press under the raw edges ½" (1.3 cm). Stitch close to the edges to create casings for the chair frame.

5   For the chair seat, cut a piece of canvas 19" × 27" (48.2 × 68.6 cm). Cut nine precut strips 27" (68.6 cm) long.

6   Arrange the strips in an interesting order and sew them to the canvas following the stitch-and-flip quilting technique (page 30). Trim the canvas to make the rectangle a finished width of 18" (45.7 cm).

7   Double-hem the long sides of the rectangle as instructed in Step 3.

8   Fold back the short sides of the rectangle 2½" (6.4 cm) and press them. Turn and press under the raw edges ½" (1.3 cm). Stitch close to the edges to create casings for the wooden sticks.

9   Insert the sticks into the chair seat casings and position the seat onto the chair. Slide the chair back casings over the chair frame.

Make it yours

- If you have a director's chair with a cover you want to replace, use the chair's existing seat and back to determine the size of the canvas rectangles to cut. Add the depth of the casings and hems to the measurements.

- If the cover is in good shape, you can rip out the hems and press it flat. Sew the strips to the canvas pieces using the stitch-and-flip quilting technique (page 30). Make sure that you have evenly positioned the strips onto the pieces.

- Make pillows from coordinating strips to create a custom look and tie the chair into the room's décor.

MODERN PATCHWORK PILLOW AND LAMPSHADE

Courtyard steps is the name of a variation of the traditional log cabin quilt block. Using fabrics with a unique color scheme will take this time-honored patchwork pattern in a modern direction. A coordinating cylinder lampshade and pillow add a contemporary touch of color to any room.

YOU WILL NEED

PRECUT FABRICS

- one 5" (12.7 cm) square
- twenty 2½" (6.4 cm) strips (10 for the pillow and approximately ten for the lampshade, depending upon its size)
- two fat quarters

OTHER SUPPLIES AND TOOLS

- 20" (50.8 cm) pillow insert
- cylinder lampshade (shade shown is 16" [40.6 cm] in diameter and 10" [25.4 cm] high)
- coordinating sewing thread
- sewing machine and iron
- usual sewing supplies
- fabric glue

PUTTING IT TOGETHER

PILLOW

Review the instructions for log cabin patchwork (page 32). This courthouse steps variation is very similar. You sew contrasting vertical and horizontal strips around a center square. Rather than sew the strips around the square from top to right side to bottom to left side, you sew the strips to each side and then to the top and bottom.

1 To make the front of the pillow, select 10 precut strips, 5 light and 5 dark colors. You will use light strips to sew to the sides of the center square and dark strips to sew to the top and bottom of the center square.

2 Using a ¼" (6 mm) seam allowance and following the log cabin piecing technique, sew light color strips to the sides of the center square. Press the seam allowances toward the strips.

3 Use a ¼" (6 mm) seam allowance, sew dark-color strips to the top and bottom of the center square. Press seam allowances toward the strips.

(continued)

4 Using ½" (1.3 cm) seam allowances, add another row of strips around the center square, keeping the light colors on the sides and the dark colors on the top and bottom.

5 Using ½" (1.3 cm) seam allowances, add 3 more rows of strips around the center square. The finished size of the pieced front should be 21" (53.3 cm) square. If necessary, trim it to that size.

6 The back of the pillow is made in two sections that overlap so you can easily remove the pillow insert for washing. From each fat quarter, cut a 21" × 15" (53.3 × 38.1 cm) rectangle. Press a 1" (2.5 cm) double hem along one long side of each rectangle and stitch close to the inner fold to hold the hem.

7 With the right sides together, place one back section on top of the pillow front. Align two corners and the raw edges. Place the remaining back section right sides together over the pillow front, aligning the remaining two corners and raw edges. The back sections will overlap at the center back of the pillow. Pin to hold the front to the backs and sew a ½" (1.3 cm) seam allowance around all sides of the pillow. Clip any excess fabric from the corners and turn the pillow right side out. Insert the pillow form through the overlapped back opening.

LaMPSHaDe

Make sure the lampshade you have selected has straight sides, like a drum. Measure around the top and bottom edges. They should be the same size in circumference.

1 Measure the height of the lampshade. You should cut the precut strips to that measurement minus ½" (1.3 cm). To determine the number of strips you will need to cover the shade, divide the circumference of the shade by 2 and round that number up to the next whole number. Cut the strips, reserving 4 strips to use for the top and bottom trim.

2 Arrange the cut strips in a pleasing arrangement of color and pattern. Sew them together with a ¼" (6 mm) seam allowance. To finish each seam, stitch again ⅛" (3 mm) away from the first line of stitching and trim excess fabric close to the second row of stitching. Press all seam allowances in one direction.

3 Starting at the seam of the shade, glue one short edge of the pieced strip to the lampshade. Working slowly from both top and bottom, apply lines of glue to the edges of the shade and smooth the pieced strip flat against the shade. You may find it easiest to lay the shade on its side and place a long ruler inside the shade to keep it from rolling on the work table. Glue a few inches and smooth the fabric. Then, move the ruler and roll the shade and continue to glue the fabric to the shade.

4 When you have completely covered the shade with fabric, evenly turn back the excess fabric and glue the folded edge to the shade.

5 If necessary, seam together precut strips to make a strip long enough to go around the top and bottom edges of the shade. The strips can be different coordinating prints. Fold the cut edges back ¾" (1.9 cm) to make a trim that is 1" (2.5 cm) wide. Starting at the seam, glue the folded trim to the top and bottom edges of the shade, neatly covering the raw edges of the pieced fabric. At the point where the trim ends meet, turn back the overlapping raw edge and neatly glue it in place to finish the lampshade.

5

MaKe IT Yours

- Make a smaller coordinating pillow by eliminating one or two rows of strips around the center square.

- You can make a larger pillow by adding more rows of strips around the square. You will need more precut strips for a larger pillow.

- To make a rectangular pillow, add more rows to the sides of the square to make the finished front a rectangle instead of a square. Adjust the size of the seam allowances between the rows or strips to create a pieced front that is 1" (2.5 cm) larger than the dimensions of the pillow insert.

- Baste jumbo rickrack or trim around the raw edge of the pillow front before you sew the back in place.

- If necessary to fit the circumference of the selected lampshade, adjust the width of the seam allowances when piecing the fabric strips together to cover the shade. It is okay if you trim the ending strip a little, and it is narrower than the other strips.

- The narrow seam that I have suggested for finishing the pieced fabric strips that cover the shade is optional. I chose to do it that way so the seams would look even and neat when the light shines through the shade. Depending upon the fabric colors and patterns, the seam allowances may show when the light is lit.

- Before gluing the fabric to the shade, use a lint roller to remove any stray threads on the lampshade that might show through when the light is lit.

WINDOW valance and PILLOWS

A coordinating bundle of large precut squares and a roll of precut strips make it easy to create custom room décor. The valance is the perfect topper to a window shade, and pillows carry the color and theme into the room.

YOU WILL NEED

PRECUT FABRICS

The finished dimensions of the valance shown are 15" (38.1 cm) deep and 53" (134.6 cm) wide. You may need more squares and strips if you want to make it larger. The valance should be 1½–2 times the width of the window.

- sixteen 10" (25.4 cm) charm squares
- twenty-four 2½" (6.4 cm) strips

OTHER SUPPLIES AND TOOLS

- 2¼ yd (2.1 m) pom-pom fringe
- two 18" (45.7 cm) pillow forms
- coordinating sewing thread
- sewing machine and iron
- usual sewing supplies

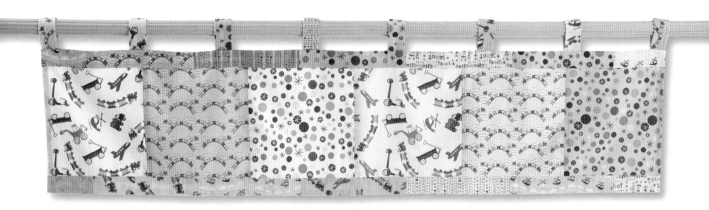

PUTTING IT TOGETHER

Use ½" (1.3 cm) seam allowance throughout the construction of the valance and pillows.

WINDOW VALANCE

1 Select six squares and sew them right sides together in a pleasing arrangement of color and pattern to make a long strip. Press the seams open.

2 Cut 26 strips each 10" (25.4 cm) long. For the top row of the valance, select seven strips and sew them right sides together. Press the seams open. Do the same for the bottom row of the valance.

3 With the right sides together, center both rows of strips to the top and bottom sides of the sewn large squares. Sew and press the seams up and down toward the strips and away from the squares. Trim excess fabric strips from each side.

4 Select six 10" (25.4 cm) strips for the hem facing. Sew them right sides together and press the seams open. With the right sides together, sew the hem facing to the bottom row of the valance. Press the seam toward the hem facing.

5 Fold and press the raw edges of the sides back ½" (1.3 cm). Fold and press them back again ½" (1.3 cm) to create a double hem. Stitch close to the inner fold line.

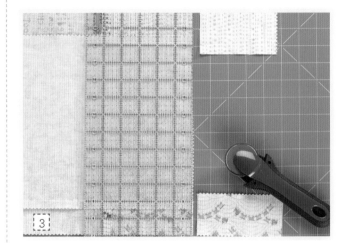

6 Fold and press the raw edge of the hem facing back ½" (1.3 cm). Align the fold line with the valance's bottom seam line and baste it in place. Stitch close to the seam line to hold.

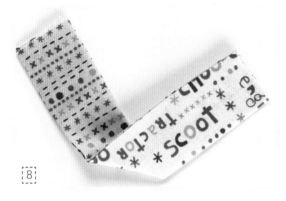

[8]

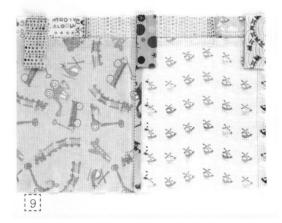

[9]

7   Sew the remaining six 10" (25.4 cm) strips together for the top facing.

8   Cut sixteen 7" (17.8 cm) lengths of strips to create the valance's eight hanging loops. Each loop can be a different color and print. To make the loops, place two strips right sides together and sew along the long edges. Turn them right side out and press them, keeping the seams along the side edges of the loops.

9   Fold the loops in half. Pin one loop at each end of the valance top and the others evenly spaced between them. The distance between the loops on the valance shown is 6" (15.2 cm). Align the raw edges of folded loops with the raw edge of the valance top. Baste the loops in place.

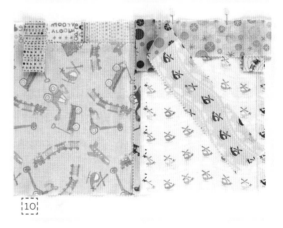

[10]

10   With the right sides together, place the top facing against the top of the valance. The side seam allowances of the facing will extend beyond the finished edge of the valance. The hanging loops will be between the layers.

11   Sew the top seam and press the seam toward the valance.

12   Press under the side seam allowances of the top facing. Fold and press the raw edge of the top facing back ½" (1.3 cm). Align the fold line with the valance top seam line and baste the fabric in place. Stitch close to the seam line to hold the fabric.

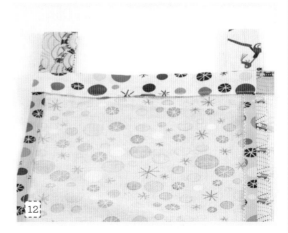

[12]

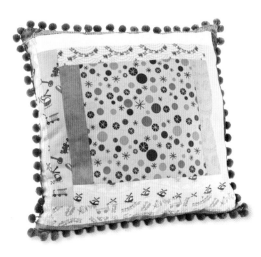

LOG CABIN PILLOW

1 Following the instructions for log cabin patchwork (page 32), construct two pieced squares for the pillow front and back. Use a large square in the middle and three rows of strips around all sides of the square. The finished size of the pieced square should be 19" (48.2 cm).

2 Baste pom-pom fringe around the right side of one of the log-cabin-pieced squares. Place the straight edge of the fringe against the raw edge of the square. Using a zipper foot, machine baste the fringe in place ½" (1.3 cm) from the edge, taking care to neatly miter the trim at the corners.

3 With the right sides together, pin the pieced squares together, aligning the raw edges. The fringe will be between the layers. Starting and ending just beyond the corners along one side, sew the squares together on three sides, leaving an opening for turning. Sew right on top of the basting stitches.

4 Trim excess fabric from the corners and turn the pillow right side out. Press back the seam allowances at the opening. Insert the pillow form and slip-stitch the opening closed.

BIG SQUARES PILLOW

1 Select four squares for the front of the pillow and four squares for the back of the pillow. With the right sides together, sew the four squares to create a large pieced square for each side of the pillow. Press seams open.

2 To make the pleated trim, sew together enough lengths of precut strips to make a piece about 6 yards (5.5 m) long. Use up leftover random lengths of strips. Sew them right

make it yours

- For a large window, make the valance wider by adding more squares to the center section and adding more 10" (25.4 cm) lengths of strips to the top and bottom rows and facings.

- To make coordinating curtains, sew a length of pieced strips to the long inner sides of two purchased window panels.

- You can trim a coordinating window shade by sewing or gluing a length of pieced strips to the lower edge of the shade.

- The pleated and pom-pom trim on the pillows is optional. You can sew them together without trim, or you can use a pieced ruffle or jumbo rickrack instead.

- Make a large floor pillow by sewing more rows around the center square of the Log Cabin Pillow or sewing strips around the four squares of the Big Square Pillow.

sides together with a ¼" (6 mm) seam allowance and press the seams open. Following the directions for making pleated trim (page 38), fold the pieced strip in half. Mark and sew ½" (1.3 cm) pleats.

3 Place the raw edge of the trim ¼" (6 mm) away from the outside edge of one of the pieced squares. Baste the trim in place along the sewn line of the pleated trim, gently curving the excess trim at the corners. Overlap the trim ends at the point where they join. Turn back a ¼" (6 mm) seam allowance so the raw edge of the top layer is not exposed.

4 With the right sides together, pin the pieced squares together, aligning the raw edges. The pleated fringe will be between the layers. Starting and ending just beyond the corners along one side, sew the squares together on three sides, leaving an opening for turning. Sew right on top of the basting stitches.

5 Trim excess fabric from the corners and turn the pillow right side out. Press back the seam allowances at the opening. Insert the pillow form and slip-stitch the opening closed.

MODULAR HEADBOARD AND ACCENT PILLOWS

Custom headboards can be very expensive but not when you grab a few fat quarters and polystyrene foam sheets. You can make the pictured headboard from modular squares that you can arrange as desired and hang them above the bed. Placed side by side, they create a padded headboard that is very light weight and can be attached to the wall with removable mounting squares, perfect for apartments and dorm rooms.

YOU WILL NEED

PRECUT FABRICS

- six fat quarters for a twin size headboard or eight for a full size headboard
- two fat quarters for the square pillow
- three fat quarters for the neck roll pillow

OTHER SUPPLIES AND TOOLS

- six 14" (356 mm) squares of high loft batting for a twin size headboard, or 8 for a full size
- two 1" x 12" x 36" (2.5 x 30.5 x 91.4 cm) polystyrene foam sheets for a twin-sized headboard or three for a full size
- one 16" (406 mm) pillow insert
- one 14" x 5" (35.6 x 12.7 cm) neck roll pillow insert
- six sheets of 12" x 12" (30.5 x 30.5 cm) cardstock for a twin size headboard or eight for a full size
- 1¾ yd (1.6 m) of ⅝" (16 mm) grosgrain ribbon
- electric knife
- ½" (1.3 cm) sequin pins
- craft glue
- ¼" (6 mm) fusible-web tape
- coordinating sewing thread
- sewing machine and iron
- usual sewing supplies

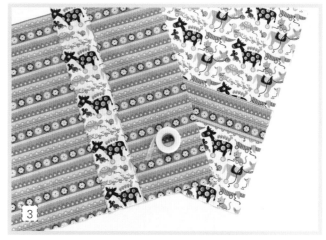

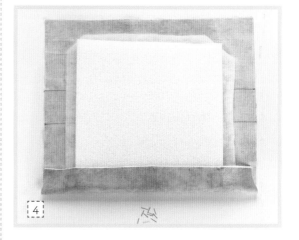

PUTTING IT TOGETHER

HEADBOARD

1. Using an electric knife, cut the foam sheets into thirds to make three 12" (30.5 cm) squares from each sheet. You will need six squares for a twin-sized headboard and eight for a full size.

2. Select six (or eight) fat quarters to cover the foam squares. Cut each into an 18" (45.7 cm) square, reserving the excess fabric strips cut from each side of the fat quarters.

3. Turn back and iron the raw edges on the excess strips to make finished strips 3" (76 mm) wide. Mixing the colors and prints, place the contrasting strips on the fat quarter squares 6" (15.2 cm) from one side. Following the manufacturer's instructions, apply fusible-web tape under the edges of the contrasting strips and iron to fuse them. This fusing eliminates the need for pins and keeps the strips straight and secure. Sew a line of stitches along each side of the strips, close to the edges.

4. To cover the foam squares, place one of the stitched fabric squares on your work surface, right side down. Center one of the batting squares onto the fabric and place a foam square onto the center of the batting. Trim the excess batting at the corners to reduce bulk.

Fold back the excess fabric along two opposite sides. Hold it in place with sequin pins. Make sure that the fabric is straight and centered onto the foam square.

5 Fold in the fabric at the corners, as you would if you were wrapping a gift box. Pin to hold it. Fold up the fabric from the remaining two sides and pin to hold them.

6 Trim the card stock into 11 ½" (29.2 cm) squares. Glue them to the back of the covered foam squares to neatly finish them. Apply removable mounting squares to the corners of each square.

7 Arrange the squares in a pleasing arrangement, creating two rows. Attach them to the wall above the bed, making sure that the edges of each square are next to each other.

square pillow

1 As described for the headboard, use two fat quarters to make the front and back of the square pillow. Trim the stitched squares to 17" (43.2 cm).

2 With the right sides together, sew the pillow front and back along three sides with a ½" (1.3 cm) seam allowance. Start and stop the stitching just inside two corners to create an opening for turning. Clip the corners. Turn the pillow right side out. Iron back the seam allowances at the opening. Insert the square pillow form and slip-stitch the opening closed.

neck roll pillow

1 Select one fat quarter for the center of the pillow and one for each side. Trim all three fat quarters to 21" × 18" (53.3 × 45.7 cm).

2 On all three rectangles, align the raw edges along the long side, right sides together. Sew each rectangle into a tube, using a ½" (1.3 cm) seam allowance. Press the seam allowances open.

3 With the right sides together, sew the side tubes onto the center tube. Press the seams toward the sides.

4 Turn back the raw edges of the side sections ½" (1.3 cm) and iron them. Fold back the side sections and align the fold line with the center section's seam line. Press. Baste or pin to hold the fabric. Stitch close to the fold line.

5 Turn the pillow right side out. Insert the neck-roll pillow form and center it inside the pillow. Cut the ribbon in half. Gather up the end sections around the ends of the pillow and tie the ribbon around the gathers to hold it. Tie each ribbon into a bow.

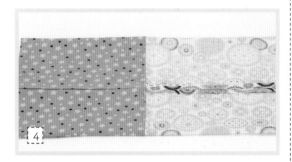

tea cozy, trivet, and tea towel

Make tea-time special with a coordinated tea cozy and trivet made from precut strips. Trim a purchased dish towel with the leftover strips.

YOU WILL NEED

PRECUT FABRICS

- fifteen to twenty 2½" (6.4 cm) strips; the actual amount will depend upon the size of your tea pot
- two fat quarters

OTHER SUPPLIES AND TOOLS

- ½ yd (.5 m) of needled, insulated lining
- 1 yd (.9 m) of fusible web
- ¼ yd (.2 m) of wool felt
- purchased dish towel, washed and dried to allow for shrinkage
- pom-pom trim, enough to go across the width of the towel plus 2" (5 cm)
- measuring tape
- paper for pattern making
- ruler and pencil
- coordinating sewing thread
- sewing machine and iron
- usual sewing supplies

PUTTING IT TOGETHER

TEA COZY

1   To make a pattern for the tea cozy, measure around your teapot at its widest point, including the handle and spout. Divide that number by 2 and add 2" (5 cm). That amount will be the width of your pattern.

2   Measure your teapot from the table up and over the highest point of the lid and back down to the table on the other side. Divide this number by 2 and add 3" (76 mm). This amount will be the height of your pattern.

3   On a piece of paper, draw a rectangle the width determined in Step 1 and the height determined in Step 2. Fold the paper in half widthwise and round the top corners of the rectangle. The edge of a dinner plate is a good curve to trace for the corner. Cut out the curved corner to create the pattern.

4   For the lining of the tea cozy, use the fat quarters and cut two rectangles a little larger than the pattern. Cut two rectangles of insulated lining and two rectangles of fusible web in the same dimensions.

5   Following the manufacturer's instructions, fuse the insulated lining to the wrong side of each fat-quarter rectangle. The shiny side of the insulated lining should be against the wrong side of the lining fabric.

6   Cut fabric strips the height of the rectangle. Cut enough strips to fit across the width, allowing for ¼" (6 mm) seam allowances. Following the stitch-and-flip quilting technique (page 30), sew the strips to the insulated lining side of both rectangles.

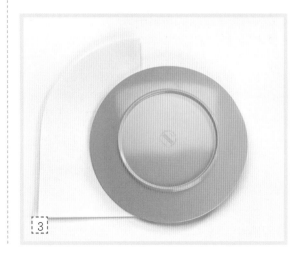

7 Center the tea-cozy pattern onto the rectangles. Pin and cut the front and back pieces of the tea cozy.

8 For the handle, cut a 6" (15.2 cm) length of one precut fabric strip. Make a stitched-and-turned strip (page 34). Press and trim the finished strip to 4" (10.1 cm). Fold the strip in half. Aligning all the raw edges, baste the handle to the top center of one of the cozy pieces.

9 Pin the front and back pieces for the tea cozy right sides together. With a ¼" (6 mm) seam allowance, sew along the curved edge. Leave the straight edge at the bottom open. Machine zigzag stitch over the raw edges of the seam allowance and turn the cozy right side out.

10 Following the instructions for binding edges (page 28), bind the bottom edge of the tea cozy.

11 If desired, make a variety of fabric flowers and leaves and handsew them around the handle.

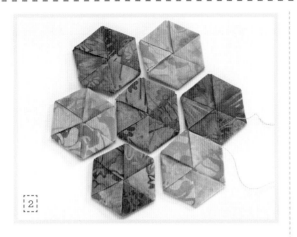

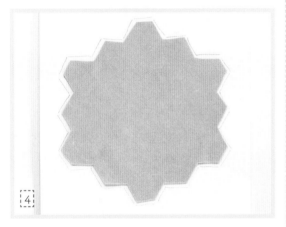

Trivet

1. Make 19 folded rosettes (page 42). Each precut fabric strip will make three rosettes. Select one fabric to make the center rosette. Use two strips to make six rosettes for the first row of rosettes sewn around the center. Use four strips to make 12 rosettes to sew around the outer edge of the trivet.

2. Slip-stitch six rosettes around the center rosette, aligning all the finished edges.

3. Slip-stitch 12 rosettes around the shape to create the outer row, aligning all the finished edges.

4. Place the trivet onto a piece of paper and trace the outline. Create a pattern for the felt backing and insulated lining by making the lines of the tracing ¼" (6 mm) smaller on all sides.

5. Place the nonshiny side of the insulated lining against the felt and cut the pattern shape. Trim the insulated lining ¼" (6 mm) smaller on all sides.

[6]

6 Position the insulated lining and the felt backing onto the back of the trivet and slip-stitch it in place.

Tea Towel

1 Make a length of fabric rickrack (page 36) long enough to go across the width of the towel. Sew the rickrack to the bottom edge of the towel.

2 Cover enough pom-pom trim (page 37) with various bits of fabric used in the tea cozy and trivet. Sew the pom-pom trim to the bottom edge of the towel.

accessories, wearables, and gifts

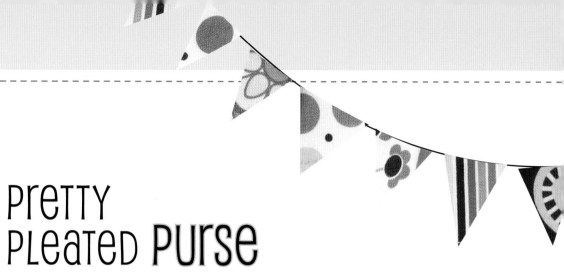

PRETTY PLEATED PURSE

Get a head start on making this pleated purse by using a plain, natural-canvas tote bag. You sew rows of pleated precut strips to the bag, and you trade in the canvas handles for decorative wooden ones. A magnetic purse clasp keeps it all together.

YOU WILL NEED

PRECUT FABRICS
- fifteen 2½" (6.4 cm) strips

OTHER SUPPLIES AND TOOLS
- 13½" × 13½" (34.3 × 34.3 cm) natural-canvas tote bag
- decorative wood purse handles; make sure that the openings of the purse handle align with the spacing of the canvas tote bag handles

- magnetic purse clasp
- coordinating sewing thread
- sewing machine and iron
- usual sewing supplies
- fabric marker
- fabric glue

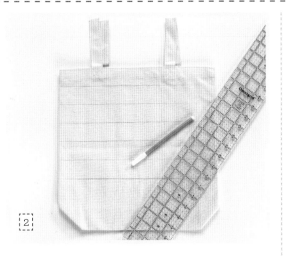

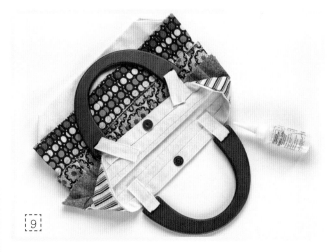

PUTTING IT TOGETHER

1 Cut off the tote bag handles 4" (10.2 cm) above the top of the bag.

2 With the fabric marker, draw a horizontal line on the tote bag 4" (10.2 cm) up and parallel from the bottom. Draw five more parallel lines, each 1½" (3.8 cm) above the last. These six lines will be the placement lines for the rows of pleated ruffles.

3 For each row of pleats, select two precut strips. Right sides together, join the short ends with a ¼" (6 mm) seam allowance. Press the seam allowance to one side. Sew a line of straight stitches ¼" (6 mm) from one long raw edge of the joined strip. This edge will be the bottom edge of the strip.

4 Following the instructions for making knife pleats (page 38), fold the strip into 1" (2.5 cm) knife edge pleats. Stitch across the top to hold the pleats in place.

5 Align the top raw edge of the pleated strip to the bottom marked line on the bag and pin, placing the end of the strip at one side seam. Pin the strip around the tote. Trim excess

fabric and turn back the raw edge of the top strip, overlapping the beginning. Sew the pleats in place over the previous stitches.

6 In the same way, sew five additional rows of pleated strips to the bag.

7 Following the manufacturer's instructions, apply both sides of the magnetic clasp to the top centers of the bag. The clasp should be on the inside of the bag and the bent-back prongs on the outside.

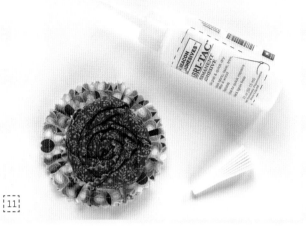

[11]

8   For the top row of the bag, cut a strip 1" (2.5 cm) longer than the bag circumference. Iron both long raw edges back ½" (1.3 cm). Glue the strip to the top of the bag, covering the top of the last row of pleats and the prongs of the magnetic clasp. Overlap the ends at one side of the bag and turn back the top end to finish them. Glue them in place.

9   Insert the cut bag handles into the openings of the decorative purse handle. Turn back the raw edges of the handles and glue them securely to the top inside of the bag.

10 Make a rolled rosette (page 46) with a 22" (55.9 cm) fabric strip.

11 Cut a 16" (406 mm) length of another fabric strip. Following the instructions for making a gathered rosette (page 40), sew the strip into a circle. Sew a line of stitching ¼" (6 mm) away from both raw edges. Press up one side 1" (2.5 cm) and gather the fabric along the folded edge to make a doubled, gathered rosette. Glue the rolled rosette to the center of the gathered rosette.

12 Glue the completed flower to the top center on one side of the bag, over the area where you have attached the clasp.

MaKe IT Yours

- It is helpful if your sewing machine has a free arm so you can reach into the canvas bag to sew the rows of pleats. If that process is difficult to do with your sewing machine, glue the rows of pleats to the bag.

- The precut fabric strips that I selected for this bag have pinked edges. I chose to finish the exposed edges of the pleated strips by sewing a line of straight stitches ¼" (6 mm) from the edge. If the edges of the fabric strips you want to use are not pinked with a zigzag edge or if you like a more finished look, iron a narrow, double hem along the edge of the pleated strip and stitch close to the fold. Or you can finish the edges of the strips with a decorative machine-overcast stitch.

- The decorative handles are optional. If desired, you can leave the canvas tote bag handles plain or cover them with a fabric strip. Press back the raw edges of a fabric strip to create a strip the width of the handle or slightly smaller. Glue or sew the fabric strip to the handles.

- Since you have covered so much of the tote bag with rows of pleats, you do not have to use a plain canvas bag. You might have an old printed tote bag that you can use as the base of the purse. This is a great project for recycling.

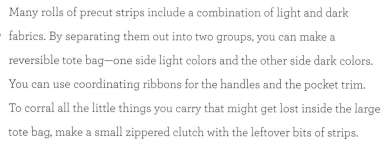

reversible
TOTE AND
CLUTCH BAG

Many rolls of precut strips include a combination of light and dark fabrics. By separating them out into two groups, you can make a reversible tote bag—one side light colors and the other side dark colors. You can use coordinating ribbons for the handles and the pocket trim. To corral all the little things you carry that might get lost inside the large tote bag, make a small zippered clutch with the leftover bits of strips.

YOU WILL NEED

PRECUT FABRICS

- twenty 2½" (6.4 cm) strips (ten light colors and ten dark colors)
- twelve 6" (15.2 cm) squares (six light colors and six dark colors) for pockets
- one fat quarter for the clutch's lining

OTHER SUPPLIES AND TOOLS

- 2⅛ yd (1.9 meters) of 1½" (3.8 cm) coordinating ribbon, light color
- 2⅛ yd (1.9 meters) of 1½" (3.8 cm) coordinating ribbon, dark color
- 20" × 36" (50.8 × 91.4 cm) rectangle of Roc-Lon® Multi-Purpose Cloth or heavyweight nonfusible interfacing
- 20" × 36" (50.8 × 91.4 cm) rectangle of thin cotton batting
- ½" (1.3 cm) strips of fusible web
- two 6½" × 10½" (16.5 × 26.7 cm) rectangles of fusible fleece
- 12" (30.5 cm) or longer zipper for clutch
- ¾" (1.9 cm) D-ring and swivel clasp
- coordinating sewing thread
- sewing machine and iron
- usual sewing supplies

PUTTING IT TOGETHER

reversible TOTE

Use ½" (1.3 cm) seam allowances throughout construction of tote, unless instructed otherwise.

1 Cut 36" (91.4 cm) lengths of the 20 strips and separate them into two piles—light colors and dark colors.

2 Following the instructions for stitch-and-flip quilting (page 30), sew the dark-colored strips to the Multi-Purpose Cloth or heavyweight interfacing. Sew the light-colored strips to the cotton batting. Trim the rectangles to the same size and check that all sides are straight. The shorter sides of the rectangles will be the top edges of the tote. Fold the rectangles in half and mark the center line on the wrong side with a pencil or fabric marking pen. This area will be the bottom of the tote.

3 To make the pockets, sew the six dark-colored squares together in two rows of three squares each. In the same way, sew the six light-colored squares together.

4 Fold the pockets in half and decide which side will be the front of each; unfold. Position a dark ribbon onto the front of the dark pocket and light ribbon onto the light pocket, centering the ribbons over the horizontal seams. Use strips of fusible web to hold the ribbons in place. Sew the ribbons to the pockets.

5 Fold each pocket in half, right sides together. Starting at the fold line, sew along the sides, leaving an opening for turning.

6 Clip the corners and turn the pockets right side out. Iron the pockets, making sure to press under the seam allowances at the openings.

7 Center the light pocket onto the light side of the tote bag with the top of the pocket 4" (10.2 cm) from the raw edge. Stitch the pocket to the tote bag, close to the sides and bottom

edges. Do the same with the dark pocket on the dark side of the tote.

8 Fold the light side of the tote bag, right sides together; sew the side seams. Press the seams open. Repeat for the dark side.

9 To shape the bottom of the tote, align the side seams with the marked center line. Flatten the triangle formed and stitch straight across it, 1¾" (4.5 cm) from the point. Repeat for both pieces. Slip-stitch the triangles to the bottom of the bag.

10 To make the handles, cut each remaining ribbon into two equal lengths. You will have four ribbon lengths—two light and two dark.

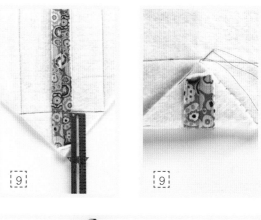

With the wrong sides together, fuse the light ribbons to the dark ribbons. Sew close to the long edges with your machine's straight, zigzag, or blanket stitches.

11 Position the light side of the handles against the light sides of the tote. Align the raw edges of the handles with the top edge of the tote. Place the outer edge of the handles 4" (10.2 cm) in from each side seam. Baste the edges to hold them.

12 Place the right side of the light side of the tote against the right side of the dark side. The sides with the pockets should be against the sides without the pockets. Align the raw edges, matching the side seams. Stitch the top edges together, leaving an opening for turning.

13 Turn the tote right side out through the opening. Push the light side of the bag into the dark side. Iron the top edge of the tote, making sure to press back the seam allowances of the opening. Slip-stitch the opening

closed. Hand baste close to the top edge to hold the layers together. Using a heavy machine needle, top stitch ¼" (6 mm) from the finished edge. Remove the basting stitches.

CLUTCH BAG

1 Cut two 6½" × 10½" (16.5 × 26.7 cm) rectangles from the fat quarter for the bag lining. Following manufacturer's instructions, iron the fusible-fleece rectangles to the back of the fabric rectangles.

2 From leftover strips used for tote bag, cut ten 6½" (16.5 cm) strips. If you like, you can divide them in half and use the light colors for one side of the clutch and dark colors for the other side. Following the instructions for stitch-and-flip quilting (page 30), sew five strips to the fleece side of each rectangle. Trim the rectangles to the same size, even with the edge of the fabric strips.

3 Cut two 1½" (3.8 cm) lengths of strips to cover the ends of the zipper. Fold each in half lengthwise, wrong sides together, and press them. Press the raw edges to meet at the center crease. Refold and press again.

4 Stitch across the zipper teeth near the zipper stop at the bottom of the zipper. Cut the zipper stop off. Unzip the zipper several inches. Trim the zipper 1" (2.5 cm) shorter than the top measurement of the bag sections. Make sure not to cut off the zipper pull.

5 Insert the ends of the zipper into the folded strips and stitch close to the fold. Trim excess fabric even with the edge of the zipper.

6 With the right sides together, center the zipper on the top of one bag section. The zipper pull faces the right side of the pieced rectangle

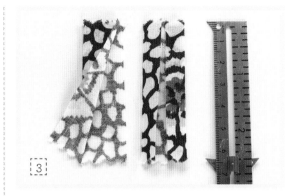

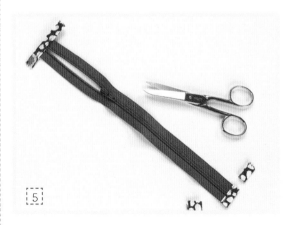

and the edge of the zipper aligns with the edge of the rectangle. Use a zipper foot and stitch the zipper to the top of the bag with a

¼" (6 mm) seam allowance. Finish the seam with a zigzag stitch to prevent the raw edges of the fabric from raveling.

7   Fold the bag section away from the zipper and pin. Topstitch close to the fold to hold the zipper tape in place.

8   Repeat Steps 6 and 7 to attach the second bag section to the other side of the zipper.

9   To make the handle and loop for the D-ring, cut a 16" (40.6 cm) strip of fabric. If necessary, sew together two or three leftover pieces to make a long-enough strip. Fold the strip in half lengthwise, with the wrong sides together, and press it. Press raw edges to meet at the center crease. Refold and press again. Stitch close to both sides.

10 Cut a 2½" (6.4 cm) length of the finished strip and insert it into the D-ring. Line up the raw edges and stitch close to form the loop. Align the raw edges of the loop with the right side of one edge of the bag, about ½" (1.3 cm) down from the zipper. Stitch a scant ¼" (6 mm) to hold.

11 Unzip the zipper halfway. Fold the bag right sides together. Sew a ¼" (6 mm) seam along the sides and the bottom of the bag. Make sure the tab and the previous stitching lines are caught in the side seams. Zigzag the edges of the seam allowance together to prevent raveling.

12 If you would like to shape the bottom of the clutch, align the side seams with the bottom seam. Flatten the triangles formed at each side and stitch straight across them, 1" (2.5 cm) from the point.

13 Turn the clutch right side out. To make the handle, slide the swivel clasp onto the remainder of the strip sewn in Step 9. Fold under one raw end ¼" (6 mm). Slip the opposite end underneath and stitch across all layers to hold them. Clip the handle onto the D-ring.

HOBO BaG

You'll need five coordinating fat-quarter prints to make this soft hobo-style bag. You use two fat quarters for the outside and two for the lining. You use the fifth one to make the handles and an inside divided pocket.

YOU WILL NeeD

PRECUT FABRICS

- five fat quarters

OTHER SUPPLIES AND TOOLS

- 9" (22.9 cm) round dinner or paper plate
- polyester fiberfill
- long pencil or dowel
- 14" (35.6 cm) of ¾" (1.9 cm) elastic
- large safety pin
- coordinating sewing thread
- sewing machine and iron
- usual sewing supplies

PUTTING IT TOGETHER

Use ½" (1.3 cm) seam allowances throughout the construction of the bag.

1 Iron all fat quarters and set one aside for the handle and inside pocket. Place the fat quarters for the lining right sides together. On top of the lining pieces, place the outside fat quarters right sides together. With a rotary cutter and ruler, trim the four fat quarters to the same exact size. Make sure all the sides are straight and parallel. Trim away the selvage edges.

2 From the fifth fat quarter, cut two 3" × 22" (7.6 × 55.9 cm) rectangles for the handles. Set aside. For the pocket, fold the remainder of the fat quarter in half lengthwise, with the right sides together, and stitch along the long edge, forming a tube. Turn the tube right side out and press it, keeping the seam line along the edge.

3 Place the pocket onto one of the lining fat quarters, 2½" (6.4 cm) from one long side.

(continued)

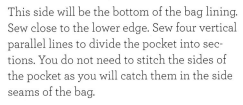

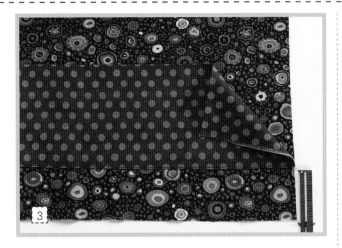

This side will be the bottom of the bag lining. Sew close to the lower edge. Sew four vertical parallel lines to divide the pocket into sections. You do not need to stitch the sides of the pocket as you will catch them in the side seams of the bag.

4   To form the curved lower edges of the bag, place the right sides of the lining pieces together. Position the dinner plate in the corner so that the edges touch the sides and bottom of the lining pieces. Trace the curved edge onto each bottom corner and trim away the excess fabric. Do the same with the outside pieces.

5   On both lining and outside pieces, mark three points on each side 2" (5 cm), 3" (7.6 cm) and 5" (12.7 cm) from the top straight edge.

6   With the outside pieces right sides together, sew around the sides and bottom of the bag from one 5" (12.7 cm) mark to the other 5" (12.7 cm) mark. Clip the seam allowances at the curves so that they will lie flat when you turn the bag right side out. Do the same with the lining pieces, leaving a 6" (15.2 cm) opening at the bottom for turning.

7 Turn the outside of the bag right side out. Place the lining over the outside, right sides together. Pin the top edges of the lining to the outside on each side of the bag. Pin the sides together from the 5" (12.7 cm) marks up to the top. Sew the lining to the bag at the upper sides and top. Leave an opening in the stitching between the 2" (5 cm) and 3" (7.6 cm) marks. This creates the casing at the top of the bag. Trim excess fabric from corners and turn the bag right side out through the lining opening. Slip-stitch the opening closed and push the lining into the bag.

8 To form the casing, sew two lines of stitches 1½" (3.8 cm) and 2½" (6.4 cm) from the top finished edge of both sides of the bag.

9 Fold each handle piece in half lengthwise, with right sides together. Stitch along the long edge, leaving the ends open. Turn the handles right side out. Stuff each handle with fiberfill, leaving the ends free of fiberfill. Use a long pencil or dowel to push the fiberfill firmly into the handles.

10 Sew across the ends of the handles. Cut the elastic into two 7" (17.8 cm) lengths. Overlap ½" (1.3 cm) of one end of each elastic length over one end of each handle and stitch it securely.

11 Attach a large safety pin to the ends of the elastic and thread each handle through each casing.

12 Overlap the remaining elastic and handle ends and stitch. Pull the elastic into the casing to cover the stitched ends. Sew the ends of both casings ¼" (6 mm) from the edges to hold the handles in place.

easy, Breezy
LITTLE GIRL'S DRESS

You can make this loose-fitting, pillowcase-style dress from less than one roll of precut strips. You can sew optional pockets from matching charm squares. Wear it as a sundress or layer it over a t-shirt and leggings.

YOU WILL NEED

PRECUT FABRICS

- one roll of 2½" (6.4 cm) strips; the exact amount of strips you will need to make the dress will depend upon the size you are making and the width of the fabric strips.
- four 5" (12.7 cm) charm squares (for optional pockets)

OTHER SUPPLIES AND TOOLS

- 2½ yd (2.3 m) of ⅝" (16 mm) satin ribbon
- one package of ⅞" (2.2 cm)-wide, single-fold, bias tape
- coordinating sewing thread
- sewing machine and iron
- usual sewing supplies
- paper for tracing armhole pattern
- safety pin

PUTTING IT TOGETHER

Unless instructed otherwise, the seam allowances are ¼" (6 mm). To finish all seams, iron seam allowances to one side and topstitch them ⅛" (3 mm) from the seam line.

You can make the dress in three sizes—small (size 3–4), medium (size 5–6) and large (7–8).

1 Cut fabric strips for the body of the dress. For the small size, you will need 18 strips cut 16" (40.6 cm) long. For the medium size, you will need 20 strips cut 21" (53.3 cm) long. And for the large size, you will need 22 strips cut 25" (63.5 cm) long.

2 Divide strips in half for the front and back of the dress. Arrange the strips in an attractive arrangement of color and pattern and sew them together to make rectangles for the dress front and back.

3 Measure the width of the pieced rectangles. Cut six fabric strips that measurement for the front and back hemline bands. Sew three strips to the lower edge of the front and back rectangles. It is okay to mix and match the strips so that they are different colors and prints on the front and the back of the dress.

(continued)

4 Trace the pattern for the size of dress you are making. Cut out the shaped armholes at the top corners of both the front and back pieces.

5 Stitch the front to the back at side seams. To finish the armholes, cut a length of bias tape long enough to go around each armhole. Press the bias tape flat. Fold the tape in half lengthwise, keeping the raw edges even and press.

6 On outside, pin the bias tape to the armhole edge, aligning the raw edges. Stitch the armhole with a 3/8" (1 cm) seam.

7 Trim the seam and clip the curves. Turn the bias tape to the inside of the dress and press. Baste it close to the inner edge. On the outside, topstitch 1/4" (6 mm) from the edge.

8 For the top casings, cut two lengths of bias tape long enough to go across the top of the front and back of the dress plus 1" (2.5 cm). Press open one folded edge.

9 Pin the tape to the upper edge of the front and back, having raw edges even and turning under ends at the armhole edges. Stitch a 3/8" (1 cm) seam.

10 Trim the seam. Turn the casing to the inside and press it. Stitch close to the inner edge.

11 Cut the ribbon in half for ties. Using a safety pin, insert the ribbons through the front and back casings, having the ends extend evenly beyond each armhole edge. Tie the ribbon ends into a bow at each shoulder when you wear the dress. If necessary, trim the ends of the ribbon to the desired length.

12 To bind the hem of the dress, select a fabric strip to go around the lower edge. If necessary, it is okay to piece that strip. Starting at one side seam, sew the strip to the bottom of the dress. Turn back the beginning short end of the strip and place the raw edge underneath where the ends of the strip overlap.

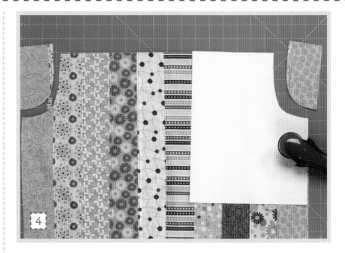

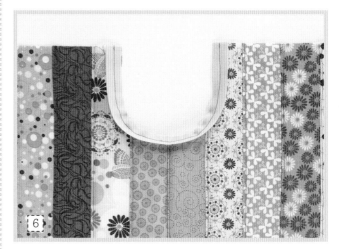

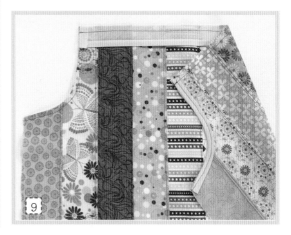

[13]

MAKE IT YOURS

• Make the dress longer or shorter by adjusting the cut length of the vertical strips or the number of strips used for the hem band.

13 Press under the raw edge of the hem binding ¼" (6 mm). Fold the binding in half and align the turned-back edge with the dress seam line. Baste. From the outside, sew a line of stitches ⅛" (3 mm) from the seam line, catching the binding edge.

14 If you desire pockets, place two charm squares right side together and stitch around the edges, leaving an opening for turning. Clip the corners and turn the fabric right side out. Press it. Position pockets on the front of the dress and stitch close to the sides and bottom of each pocket.

SMALL

MEDIUM

LARGE

roll and ruffle skirt

A roll of precut strips and a bit of elastic is all you need to stitch up this ruffled, patchwork skirt for a special little girl. Make sure to save the leftover strips to make coordinating accessories.

YOU WILL NEED

PRECUT FABRICS

- one roll of 2½" (6.4 cm) strips; the exact number of strips will depend upon the size of skirt you want to make.

OTHER SUPPLIES AND TOOLS

- ¾" (1.9 cm) of nonroll elastic the length of the child's waist plus 1" (2.5 cm)
- large safety pin
- coordinating sewing thread
- sewing machine and iron
- usual sewing supplies

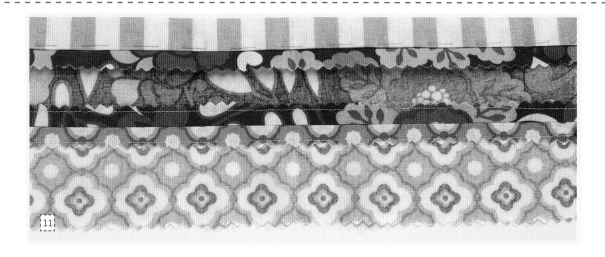

PUTTING IT TOGETHER

Unless instructed otherwise, use ½" (1.3 cm) for the seam allowances.

1   Determine the desired length of the skirt and subtract 3" (76 mm) to allow for the ruffle and seam allowances. This amount will be the length of the precut strips you will need to cut for the body of the skirt.

2   Measure the child's waist and multiple it by 1.75 times fullness. Divide that number by 1½" (3.8 cm), which is the width of one strip after seaming. If necessary, round that number up to the next whole digit. This calculation will give you the number of strips that you will cut for the body of the skirt. I made the skirt shown for a 20" (50.8 cm) waist, which requires up to 24 strips—20" × 1.75 = 35" ÷ 1½" = 23.3 (50.8 cm × 1.75 = 88.9 cm ÷ 3.8 cm = 23.4), which rounds up to 24 strips.

3   Cut the number of strips determined in Step 2 by the length determined in Step 1. Mixing patterns and colors for a random patchwork effect, place the strips in the order to be sewn.

4   Sew the strips together, creating a patched rectangle. Press the seams open and topstitch ¼" (6 mm) away from all the seams.

5   Sew the first strip to the last, forming a tube. Press the seam open and topstitch as done on the other seams.

6   To make the ruffle, measure around the edge of the patched skirt. Multiply that measurement by 1.5 and add 1" (2.5 cm). For my skirt, the calculations are 36" × 1.5 = 54" + 1" = 55" (91.4 cm × 1.5 = 137.1 cm + 2.5 cm = 139.6 cm) Sew together strips in a variety of lengths and create three ruffle sections equal to that measurement. If desired, use different colors for each ruffle section. My skirt has one section that is pink, one that is red, and one that is yellow. You should press all seams open and topstitch them as done for the body of the skirt.

7   Sew the short lengths of each ruffle section together, creating three tubes.

[12]

[13]

8   Determine which of the three sections will be the hem. Sew the remaining two ruffle sections together. Press and topstitch the seam.

9   Sew the hem section of the ruffle to the other part of the ruffle. Press the seam open.

10   Press the raw edge of the hem up ½" (1.3 cm).

11   On the wrong side, iron the fold line back to meet the seam line. Baste the fabric close to the fold.

12   Topstitch on each side of the hem ruffle seam.

13   Fold the ruffle in half and mark the folds with a pin. Starting at each pin, sew two rows of long gathering stitches at the top edge of the ruffle—one ½" (1.3 cm) from the edge and the second ¼" (6 mm).

14   Fold the skirt in half and mark the folds with a pin. With the right sides together, pin the ruffle to the bottom of the skirt, matching the pin marks to the ends of the gathering stitches. Pull the stitches to gather the ruffle and pin it, distributing the ruffle fullness evenly. Sew the ruffle to the bottom of the skirt.

(continued)

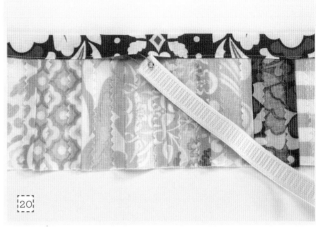

15 Press the ruffle seam up and topstitch the seam allowance to the skirt.

16 For the waistband, cut a strip the measurement of the top of the skirt plus 1" (2.5 cm). If necessary, piece together strips to create a band that measurement.

17 Sew the short ends of the waistband together, forming a tube. Press and topstitch it.

18 With the right sides together, pin the waistband to the top of the skirt. Sew it, using a ¼" (6 mm) seam allowance.

19 Press the seam allowance toward the waistband. Press the remaining raw edge of the waistband under ¼" (6 mm) and iron the fold down to meet the seam line. Pin and stitch the fabric close to the fold, leaving a 3" (76 mm) opening for inserting the elastic.

20 Attach the safety pin to one end of the elastic and thread it through the waistband.

21 Remove the safety pin. Overlap the ends of the elastic and stitch it securely.

22 Distribute the fullness evenly around the skirt. Sew the opening closed.

Make it Yours

- You can make an adult-size skirt without the ruffle. In step 2, use the widest hip measurement and add 4" (10.2 cm). Cut the strips the desired length of the skirt. Finish the hem in the same way you would finish the ruffle hem.

- Add two or three rows of strips or patched squares to the lower edge of the skirt to create a horizontal band. Finish the hem as you would for the ruffle hem.

- You can use coordinating charm squares to make patch pockets. Sew two squares right side together, leaving an opening. Trim, turn, and topstitch the side and bottom edges of the pockets to the skirt.

- Use leftover scraps to make a headband. Measure a ½" (1.3 cm) headband and cut a strip that length plus 1½" (3.8 cm). With the right sides together, sew the strip into a tube. Turn and press it. Insert the head band into the finished tube. Tuck the raw edges inside the tube and slip-stitch to close the ends. Make a raggedy rosette with a 14" (35.6 cm) fabric strip (page 41) and loopy leaves (page 45). Attach them to the headband with fabric glue.

- You also can attach a gathered or raggedy rose to a barrette or a pair of flip-flops.

SNUGGLE BLANKET AND SOFT BLOCKS

Use precut squares and strips and minky fabric to make a cuddly blanket for a special little one. Minky (sometimes spelled minkee) fabric is an incredibly soft microfiber, plush fabric. Technically, this blanket is not a quilt since it has no batting between the layers or binding around the edges. You construct the project with a simple stitch-and-turn construction.

YOU WILL NEED

PRECUT FABRICS

- thirty 6" (15.2 cm) charm squares for the quilt
- four 2½" (6.4 cm) strips
- twelve 6" (15.2 cm) charm squares for each block

OTHER SUPPLIES AND TOOLS

- 1 yd (.9 m) of minky fabric or fleece for backing
- ⅓ yd (.3 m) of heavyweight, fusible, craft interfacing for each block
- ⅓ yd (.3 m) of fusible web for each block
- die-cutting machine for cutting fabric appliqués for blocks
- polyester fiberfill
- coordinating sewing thread
- sewing machine and iron
- usual sewing supplies

SEWING WITH MINKY FABRIC

Although minky fabric is stretchy, it is not difficult to sew if you follow these tips.

- Use lots of pins to hold the fabric and minky backing together; every inch or so is not too close. These pins will force you to sew slowly around the blanket, as you do not want to sew over the pins. This sewing really does not take as long as you might think, and it will prevent the backing from stretching.

- Use a walking foot, if your sewing machine has one, to keep the stitches even.

- Do not iron minky. Press the blanket from the fabric side, taking care that the iron is not too hot.

- When sewing the quilting stitches, work from the center rows out, using a few pins to hold the patchwork flat against the backing.

PUTTING IT TOGETHER

BLANKET

The finished size of the blanket is 30½" × 36" (77.5 × 91.4 cm).

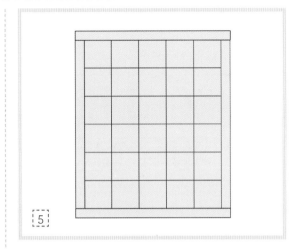

1   On your work surface, arrange the 30 charm squares in an attractive arrangement of colors and prints. Make a rectangle with six rows of five squares each.

2   Sew the blocks together in each row, using a ¼" (6 mm) seam allowance. Press the seams in one direction, alternating the direction of each row.

3   With a ¼" (6 mm) seam allowance, join the rows to make the patchwork center of the blanket. Press the seams in one direction.

4   Sew a strip to each side of the patchwork. Trim excess fabric from the ends of the strips even with the patchwork. Press the seam allowances toward the strips.

5   Sew a strip to the top and bottom sides of the patchwork. Trim excess fabric from the ends and press the seam allowances toward the strips.

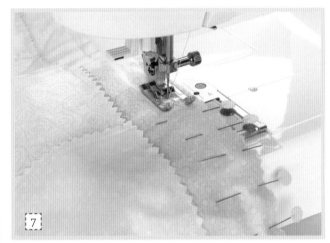

6   Smooth the backing fabric flat on your work surface, right side up. Make sure that it does not hang off the end of the table to prevent stretching. Place the patchwork on top of the backing, right side down. Keep the edge of the patchwork parallel with the selvage edge of the fabric. Pin the patchwork to the fabric around all sides. Trim the fabric even with the edges of the patchwork.

7   Minky fabric is stretchy and can shift when being sewn. Place pins every 1"–2" (2.5–5 cm) around all sides of the patchwork. Stitch the patchwork to the backing with a ½" (1.3 cm) seam allowance. Sew slowly and remove the pins as you sew. Do not sew over the pins. Leave a 6" (15.2 cm) opening along one side for turning the blanket right side out.

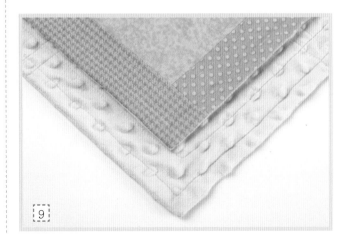

8 Clip the corners and turn the blanket right side out. Fold under the seam allowances at the opening edges and slip-stitch the opening closed. Press the blanket, taking care that the hot iron does not touch the minky backing.

9 Sew around all sides of the blanket, ½" (1.3 cm) from the finished edges. Sew quilting lines ¼" (6 mm) from both sides of all seam lines to quilt the blanket to the backing.

BLOCKS

The finished size of blocks is 5" (12.7 cm) square.

1 Select six squares for the sides of each block. Cut six 4¾" (12 cm) squares of interfacing. Following manufacturer's instructions, center and fuse an interfacing square onto the back of each fabric square.

2 Select six squares for the fabric appliqués. Apply fusible web to the back of each fabric square. With a die-cutting machine or by hand, cut various 4" (10.2 cm) letters, numbers, and shapes for each side of the block. Following the appliqué instructions (page 33), sew the appliqués to the squares.

3 Line up four squares for the sides of the block. Sew them together, using a ½" (1.3 cm) seam allowance. Start and stop the stitching on each of the four side seams ½" (1.3 cm) from the top and bottom edges.

4 Press the seams open. Sew a square to the top of the block, starting and stopping the stitching ½" (1.3 cm) from the corners.

5 The remaining square will be the bottom of the block. Press under the ½" (1.3 cm) seam allowance along the two adjoining sides. Sew the other two sides to the sides of the block, starting and stopping the stitching ½" (1.3 cm) from the corners.

6 Turn the sewn block right side out. Stuff it with fiberfill. Slip-stitch the open sides of the bottom square to the sides of the block.

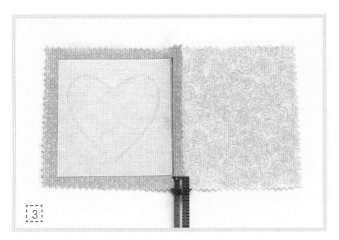

3

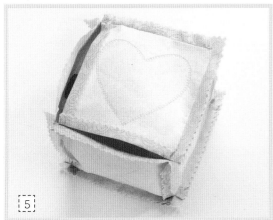

5

I Love Sleepovers
Duffle Bag and
Pillow Case

Sleepovers are fun, whether at a friend's house or on a trip to Grandma's. Why not make a special duffle bag for the occasion, with a matching pillow case? Using a die or electric fabric cutter allows you to use both positive and negative shapes for the appliquéd hearts that decorate the bag. Coordinating fat quarters and strips mixed together gives a different appearance to each side of the bag and pillow case.

YOU WILL NEED

PRECUT FABRICS FOR THE DUFFLE BAG

- six fat quarters
- twelve 6" (15.2 cm) charm squares
- six 2½" (6.4 cm) strips

PRECUT FABRICS FOR THE PILLOW CASE

- four fat quarters
- two 2½" (6.4 cm) strips

OTHER SUPPLIES AND TOOLS

- die-cutting machine cutter with heart shape
- four 6" (15.2 cm) squares fusible web
- coordinating sewing thread
- large safety pin
- sewing machine and iron
- usual sewing supplies

PUTTING IT TOGETHER

Use ½" (1.3 cm) seam allowances throughout construction of the bag and pillow case.

DUFFLE BAG

1 Select four charm squares for the contrast heart appliqués. Iron fusible web to the back of each.

2 Following the manufacturer's instructions, cut a 3½" (8.9 cm) heart from the center of each square. You will use both the cut-out heart and the remaining outside fabric as appliqués.

3 Following the appliqué instructions (page 33), fuse and sew the hearts and the squares with the cut-out hearts onto the centers of the remaining eight squares.

4 To make the front and back of the bag, sew four squares together, alternating colors. Press the seams open and topstitch them.

5 Sew a strip to the top and the bottom of the sewn squares. Trim excess fabric from ends. Press the seams open and topstitch them.

6 For the bottom of the front and back of the bag, select two fat quarters and cut a rectangle 5" × 21" (12.7 × 53.3 cm) from each. Save the remainder of the fat quarters for the bottom of the bag lining. Sew the rectangles to the bottom strips of both the front and back of the bag. Press the seams open and topstitch them.

7 Sew the long side of a fat quarter to the top strips of the front and back of the bag. Trim excess fabric straight, if necessary. Press the seams open and topstitch them.

8 To make the lining for each side of the bag, sew the long side of a fat quarter to the remainder of the fat quarter cut in Step 6. Press the seams open.

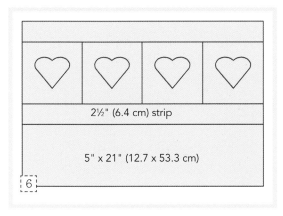

2½" (6.4 cm) strip

5" x 21" (12.7 x 53.3 cm)

6

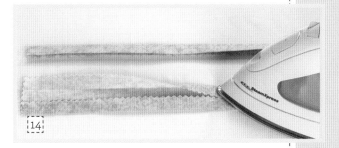

14

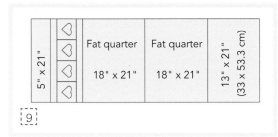

5" x 21"

Fat quarter
18" x 21"

Fat quarter
18" x 21"

13" x 21"
(33 x 53.3 cm)

9

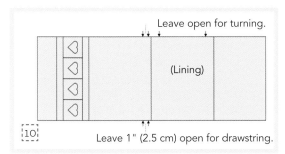

Leave open for turning.

(Lining)

Leave 1" (2.5 cm) open for drawstring.

10

9 Sew the linings to the top of each side of the bag. Press the seams open. Trim excess fabric straight, if necessary, to create one long rectangle.

10 Place the front and back of bag right sides together and pin them. Stitch around the bag, leaving a large opening in the lining for turning and leaving two small openings, one on each side at the top of the bag, for the draw-string casing. The casing openings should be

1" (2.5 cm) long and begin ½" (1.3 cm) from the top seam that joins the bag and lining.

11 Clip excess fabric from the corners; turn the bag and lining right side out. Press seam allowances under at the lining opening and slip-stitch the opening closed.

12 Push the bag lining into the bag. Press the seam between the bag and lining at the top edge. Topstitch ¼" (6 mm) from the edge.

13 To form the drawstring casing, stitch again 1½" (3.8 cm) from the top edge, making sure the inside seam allowances are open and flat.

14 To make the drawstrings, iron the remaining two strips in half. Press the cut edges to the center folded edge of each strip. Fold the strip in half and press it.

15 Sew close to the long side of each folded strip.

16 Attach the safety pin to the end of one draw-string and thread it through the casing, begin-ning and ending at one side. Overlap the raw edges of the drawstring and stitch them. Pull the drawstring through the casing so that you hide the overlap.

17 Starting from the opposite side, thread the second drawstring through the casing. Overlap the ends, stitch and pull the drawstring through the casing so the ends do not show.

18 Close the bag by pulling on both drawstrings to tightly gather up the bag opening.

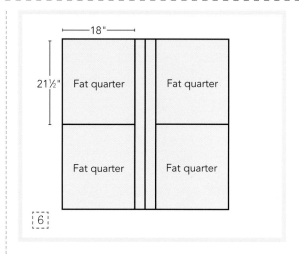

	18"	
Fat quarter		Fat quarter
Fat quarter		Fat quarter

21½"

6

PILLOW CASE

1   Trim all fat quarters to 18" × 21½" (45.7 × 54.6 cm).

2   Select two fat quarters for the top section of the pillow case. Sew them together along the short side. Stitch again ¼" (6 mm) from the seam line. Trim the fabric close to the stitching line. Zigzag stitch over the raw edge. Press the seam allowance to one side.

3   Sew one strip to the long side of the joined fat quarters. Trim excess fabric, if necessary. Press the seam open and topstitch ¼" (6 mm) on each side of the seam.

4   Sew the second strip to the first. Trim excess fabric, if necessary. Press the seam open and topstitch ¼" (6 mm) on each side of the seam.

5   Sew the remaining two fat quarters together, as done in Step 2.

6   Sew the joined fat quarters to the second strip. Press the seam open and topstitch ¼" (6 mm) on each side of the seam.

7   With the right sides together, fold the pillowcase in half, matching the seam lines and raw edges of the fabric. Stitch across the remaining long side edge and the top end.

8   Stitch again ¼" (6 mm) from the seam line. Trim the fabric close to the stitching line. Zigzag stitch over the raw edge. Press the side seam allowance to one side.

9   To hem the pillow case, fold back the cut edge 3½" (8.9 cm) and press it. Fold it back again 3½" (8.9 cm), creating a double hem. Pin the fabric. Stitch close to the fold.

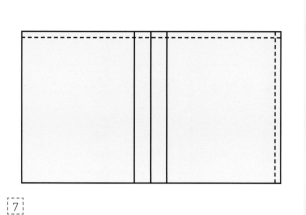

7

9

make it yours

- The duffle bag appliqués are optional. Plain squares look great too.

- You can use any shape of appliqué—stars, flower, circles, etc. Alphabet letters can spell out initials or words.

- Use pastel fabrics for a feminine look and solid neutrals for something more modern and sophisticated.

- Make coordinated mix-and-match pillow-cases to coordinate with your room décor and bed linens.

- The duffle bag also makes a great laundry bag. It's perfect to stitch up in school colors for a student going off to college.

Bargello
Yoga Mat Bag

Carry your yoga mat to class in style with this easy-to-carry shoulder bag. You construct the bag with a Bargello patchwork technique that a traditional needlework stitch inspired. The light to dark shades of color in a roll of precut strips are perfect for creating the zigzag pattern.

YOU WILL NEED

PRECUT FABRICS

- eighteen 2½" (6.4 cm) strips
- two fat quarters for the lining

OTHER SUPPLIES AND TOOLS

- 20" x 35" (50.8 x 88.9 cm) rectangle of fleece or thin batting
- two 35" (88.9 cm) lengths of 1½" (3.8 cm) ribbon to coordinate with fabrics
- ¼" (6 mm) fusible-web tape
- coordinating sewing thread
- sewing machine and iron
- usual sewing supplies

PUTTING IT TOGETHER

Use a ½" (1.3 cm) seam allowance unless instructed otherwise.

1   Cut 27" (68.6 cm) lengths from 17 of the fabric strips. Arrange the lengths in an interesting pattern of light and dark colors.

2   With a ¼" (6 mm) seam allowance, sew the strips together along the long edges to create one large pieced rectangle. Press the seam allowances in one direction toward the bottom strip.

4   Sew the remaining two long edges together, creating a cylinder of fabric with the seams on the outside. Press the remaining seam allowance in the same direction as the other seams.

5   Flatten the cylinder and trim the edge if necessary to straighten it. The cut edge should be perpendicular to the fold of the cylinder to assure that the rows of patches will be straight. Use your ruler and rotary cutter to cut rows across the cylinder. Cut one 2½" (6.4 cm)-wide strip (A), seven 2" (5 cm)-wide strips (B), two 1¾" (4.5 cm)-wide strips (C), and two 2¼" (5.7 cm)-wide strips (D).

6   Starting with an A strip, decide what fabric print you would like to have at the bottom square of the first patchwork row. Use a seam ripper to undo the seam at that point and make a long strip.

6

9

8

7 Place the first strip on your work table. Holding a B strip, locate the seam that is one row lower than the one you undid on the first strip and remove the stitches to make a long strip. This change will advance the fabric patterns up one row. Place it on your work surface next to the A strip.

8 Arrange the twelve strips cut from the cylinder in the following pattern: A, B, B, C, B, B, D, B, B, C, B, D. Cut the strips at the seams where the cut will allow the fabric patterns to advance up through strip C and then down to strip D two times.

9 Place the first strip A along the long edge of the fleece rectangle and stitch ¼" (6 mm) from the edge. Using the stitch-and-flip quilting technique (page 30), sew the remaining 11 strips to the fleece, pressing well after you sew each strip.

10 Trim excess fleece from the rectangle and make sure the edges are straight and perpendicular to each other.

(continued)

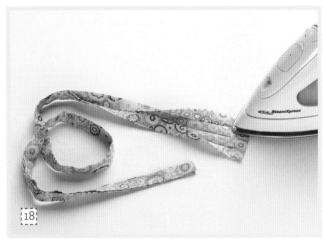

11 To make the handle, place the two ribbon lengths right sides together and sew the short edges together. Turn the ribbons right side out and press the seams. Apply strips of fusible-web tape to the edges of one of the ribbons. Following the manufacturer's instructions, fuse the two ribbons wrong sides together. Sew machine blanket or zigzag stitches along both long edges.

12 Center and pin the handle ends over the middle seam of the patchwork, 7½" (19 cm) from the bottom and 8½" (216 mm) from the top. Stitch the ends in place.

13 For the lining, sew the two fat quarters together along the long edge. Press the seam open. Trim the rectangle the same size as the patchwork rectangle.

14 With the right sides together, fold the patchwork rectangle in half lengthwise. Stitch along the bottom and side edges. Press the side seam open and turn the tube inside out.

15 Fold the lining in half lengthwise, with the right sides together. Stitch along the bottom and side edges, leaving an opening in the side seam for turning. Press the seam open.

16 Place the right side of lining against the right side of the bag. Stitch them together along the top edge.

17 Turn the bag right side out through the lining opening. Slip-stitch the opening closed. Push the lining into the bag. Iron the top edge of the bag and topstitch ¼" (6 mm) from the edge.

18 For the ties, cut a 33" (83.8 cm) length of fabric from the remaining strip. Fold up the seam allowances and press the raw edges on the short ends. Fold and press the strip in half. Fold and press the raw edges along the long edges to the center crease. Fold the strip in half and press it.

19

19 Stitch the piece close to all sides of the ties. Fold the tie in half, marking the center with a pin. Place the center over the side seam of the bag, 3" (7.6 cm) from the top edge. Stitch across the tie to hold it.

Make It Yours

- Instead of ribbon, you can make the handle for the bag from two precut strips sewn together. Before stitching, apply fusible interfacing to the wrong side of both strips to make the handle sturdy.

- Sew together leftover bits of strips to make a trim to decorate a coordinating towel or make a small zippered bag.

- Bargello patchwork makes a beautiful wall hanging or quilt. Decide the height of the piece you want to make and divide by 2 to determine the number of strips you will need. Sew the strips together into a cylinder and cut the strips across as described above. The strips can be all the same size or can vary in width. Undo the strips so that the colors and prints of the fabric will advance up and down across the piece. Sew the strips together. Quilt and bind the piece or stretch the pieced fabric over a stretcher frame to create a wall hanging.

- Bargello patchwork is a great way to use up random leftover, precut strips from other projects.

TISKET TASKET
FABRIC BASKET

Use precut fabric strips stiffened with ultraheavy fusible stabilizer to weave fabric baskets. Make a few to organize spools of thread and notions in your sewing room or use them to hold a casserole dish. (Two fat quarters make an easy matching napkin.). By varying the number of strips, you can make the baskets in many different sizes.

YOU WILL NEED

PRECUT FABRICS

To make a 6" x 6" x 3½" (15.2 x 15.2 x 8.9 cm) basket:

- ten 2½" (6.4 cm) strips

OTHER SUPPLIES AND TOOLS

- ¾ yd (.7 m) of 20" (50.8 cm)-wide, double-sided, fusible, ultrafirm stabilizer
- large safety pin
- Fasturn tool (optional but very helpful)
- fabric glue
- wooden clothes pins
- coordinating sewing thread
- sewing machine and iron
- usual sewing supplies

PUTTING IT TOGETHER

1 From the stabilizer, cut ¾" (1.9 cm) strips to stiffen the fabric tubes that you will use for weaving the basket. Cut three strips 26" (66 cm) long. Cut 12 strips 15" (38.1 cm) long.

2 Cut three fabric strips 26" (66 cm) long and 12 strips 15" long (38.1 cm). With the right sides together, sew the strips together with a ¼" (6 mm) seam allowance along the long edges to create tubes as described for making stitched and turned strips (page 34). Use the Fasturn tool or a large safety pin to turn the tubes right side out. Press each tube, with the seam along one pressed edge.

3 Use the safety pin to insert a strip of stabilizer inside each tube. Following manufacturer's instructions, fuse the stabilizer inside the tubes.

(continued)

4   Select six 15" (38.1 cm) finished strips and lay them vertically side by side on your ironing board. The total width of the strips should be 6" (15.2 cm). Pin each strip at the top to the ironing board.

5   Starting about 4½" (11.4 cm) from the bottom, weave a 15" (38.1 cm) finished strip horizontally across in an over-one-and-under-one pattern. Weave a second strip across, going over the strips you went under and under the strips you went over in the first row.

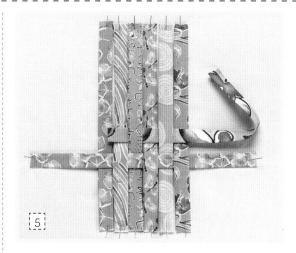

[5]

6   Continue to alternate rows and weave the remaining four 15" (38.1 cm) strips across. The woven area should be 6" (15.2 cm) square. Pin the strips together and machine-sew around the square, close to all edges of the square, to hold the rows together. Fold back the ends of all the strips toward the center of the weaving and iron.

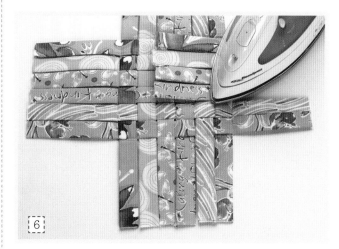

[6]

7   Trim the remaining three strips to 24½" (62.2 cm). On each strip, overlap the ends ½" (1.3 cm) and sew straight across them to create a ring. Neatly trim the excess stabilized fabric from each side of the stitching line. You will use these rings to weave the sides of the basket.

8   Place the first ring over the woven center. Position and alternate the ends of the strips coming up from the bottom of the basket so that they continue the over-and-under weaving pattern. Use clothes pins to hold the ring in place as you weave around the center. Weave the remaining two rings up the sides of the basket. Push the rows close to each other, using clothes pins to help hold the rows together. Use a small amount of fabric glue to secure each strip end to the last woven row. When the glue is dry, trim the strip ends evenly ½" (1.3 cm) above the last woven ring.

[7]

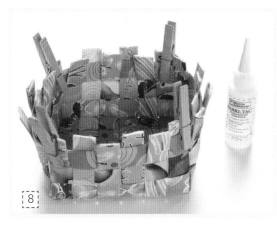

Make It Yours

- The number of strips used to weave the bottom of the basket determines the size of the basket. Make an 8" (20.3 cm)-square basket to hold a baking dish. The basket can serve as a carrier and a hot pad.

- Make a coordinated, lined napkin from two fat quarters as instructed for the Mix and Match Placemat (page 55). Place the napkin in the basket and fill it with cookies, a coffee cake, or a special treat.

- You can weave the basket as a square or a rectangle.

- Make the basket shorter or taller by weaving only two rings around the basket or by weaving more than three rings.

- To make a very large basket, you may need to piece together precut strips so that they are long enough for the side rings. To determine the length that you should cut the ring strips, measure the sides of the woven basket bottom plus ½" (1.3 cm) for the overlap.

9 Cut a 25½" (64.8 cm) length from the remaining precut strip for the top binding. Fold one short raw edge back ½" (1.3 cm) and press it. Fold the strip in half and press it. Pin the folded strip against the inside of the top edge of the basket, aligning the raw edges with the cut ends of all the strips. Starting a few inches from the folded end, sew the binding around the basket. As you approach the beginning of the stitching, slip the raw edge of the binding strip inside the folded edge and continue sewing across the piece. Fold the binding to the outside of the basket, aligning the fold line with the top edge of the last row; press. Machine or handstitch close to the fold.

MOMMY AND ME
APRONS, POT HOLDER, AND OVEN MITT

It's time for fun in the kitchen for a special mom and her little helper.
One roll of 30 precut strips and one charm pack of 30 squares will make
both aprons and the matching pot holder and oven mitt.

YOU WILL NEED

PRECUT FABRICS

- thirty 2½" (6.4 cm) strips
- thirty 6" (15.2 cm) squares

OTHER SUPPLIES AND TOOLS

- jumbo rickrack—1⅝ yd (1.5 m) for the child's apron, 2⅜ yd (2.2 m) for the adult apron
- 1½" (3.8 cm) pom-pom trim —⅝ yd (.6 m) for the child's apron, 1 yd (.9 m) for the adult apron
- 2¼" (5.7 cm) strips of midweight, fusible interfacing for the apron waistbands

- ½ yd (.5 m) of needled insulated lining for the pot holder and oven mitt
- ⅓ yd (.3 m) of fusible fleece for the oven mitt
- two fat quarters or ⅓ yd (.3 m) muslin for oven-mitt lining
- temporary fabric-adhesive spray
- 10" x 14" (25.4 x 35.6 cm) paper for oven-mitt pattern
- coordinating sewing thread
- sewing machine and iron
- usual sewing supplies

PUTTING IT TOGETHER

Unless stated otherwise, use ½" (1.3 cm) seam allowances through construction of all projects.

CHILD'S APRON

1 Select eight 6" (15.2 cm) squares to use for the skirt of the apron. Position them as desired and sew them together in two rows of four squares each. Press the seams open and topstitch.

2 Sew two strips to the bottom of the patched skirt for borders. Trim excess fabric from the ends of the border strips. Press the seams open and topstitch them.

3 Sew two rows of rickrack centered over the border seams.

4 Press a double, ½" (1.3 cm) hem at the bottom of the skirt. Sew a row of pom-pom trim under the folded hem edge. Topstitch close to the fold and again ¼" (6 mm) away.

5 Press a double, ½" (1.3 cm) hem at each side of the skirt and stitch it.

6 To make pockets, select two squares to use for the outside pockets and two for the pocket linings. For each pocket, sew a lining square to an outside pocket square, with the right sides together. Leave a small opening for turning them. Turn and press them. Position the pockets on the skirt, 3½" (8.9 cm) from the top and 2" (5 cm) from the hemmed side edges. Edgestitch the pockets in place along the sides and bottom of each pocket.

7 Sew two rows of long gathering stitching along the top edge of skirt.

8 To make the apron bib, sew one strip to each side of one square. Press the seams open and topstitch them. Sew two border strips to the top side. Trim excess fabric from the ends of the border strips. Press the seams open and topstitch them. Sew two rows of rickrack centered over the border seams. Press a ½" (1.3 cm), double hem at the sides of the bib.

8a

9

8b

10

9 For the neck strap, cut two strips 18" (45.7 cm) long. Make two stitched and turned strips (page 34).

10 Pin the short ends of the strap to the top of the bib, aligning the finished edges with the hemmed sides. Baste the strap ends to the bib.

(continued)

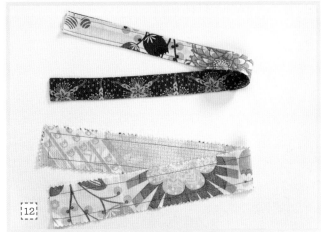

11 Press a double, ½" (1.3 cm) hem at the top edge of the bib and machine-stitch close to the fold and ¼" (6 mm) away, making sure to catch the raw edges of the neck strap in the hem.

12 For the apron ties, select four strips and cut them 26" (66 cm) long. For each tie, sew two strips with the right sides together, leaving one short end open. Trim the ties, turn them right side out, press them, and topstitch them along the sewn three sides.

13 Cut two 12" (30.5 cm) strips for the waistband and waistband lining. Cut one strip of fusible interfacing 12" (30.5 cm) long, and following manufacturer's instructions, fuse it to the back of the outside strip for the waistband. Mark the center of the waistband with a pin.

14 Matching the centers, gather the skirt to fit the interfaced waistband, leaving waistband on each side extending ½" (1.3 cm) beyond the finished sides of skirt. Adjust the gathers and pin and stitch them. Press the seam toward the waistband.

15 Pin and baste the raw ends of the ties to each side of the waistband.

16 With the right sides together, pin and baste the raw edge of the bib to the top of the waistband, making sure that the center of the bib aligns with the center of the waistband.

17 Press the raw edge under ½" (1.3 cm) on one long side of the waistband lining.

18 With the right sides together, place the waistband lining over the waistband. Pin and stitch the upper long edge and the short ends, making sure to catch both the ties and the bib in the seam.

19 Trim and turn the fabric. Pin the lining to the waistband seam and slip-stitch the turned edge over the skirt seam.

2 Use a ¼" (6 mm) seam allowance when sewing the squares together for the pockets.

3 You make the bib with seven 8" (20.3 cm) strips. Stitch them together, press the seams open, and topstitch them. Sew two border strips to the top and add rickrack.

4 Cut the strips for the neck strap 23" (58.4 cm) long.

5 Use the full length of the strips selected for the ties.

6 Cut the waistband and the waistband lining strips 19" (48.2 cm) long.

HOT PAD

1 Cut two 10" (25.4 cm) squares of needled, insulated lining.

2 On one square, sew five strips together using the stitch-and-flip quilting technique (page 30). Trim the sewn square to 9½" × 9½" (24.1 × 24.1 cm).

3 On the second square, center the precut square. Using the stitch-and-flip technique (page 30), sew a strip to each side of the square. Then sew strips to the top and bottom of the square. Trim the sewn square to 9½" × 9½" (24.1 × 24.1 cm), keeping the border strips the same width around the center square.

4 To make the hanger loop, cut a strip 5" (12.7 cm) long. Fold it in half and press it. Fold the raw edges to the center fold and press them.

5 Stitch close to the fold on both sides of the loop.

ADULT APRON

You construct the adult apron in the same basic way as the child's apron. Follow the previous instructions with the following changes for the size and placement of the strips and squares.

1 Make the skirt of the adult apron with twenty-one 16" (40.6 cm) strips. Stitch them together, press the seams open, and topstitch them. As for the child's apron, add two border strips and rickrack. Double-hem the bottom of the skirt and add pom-pom trim.

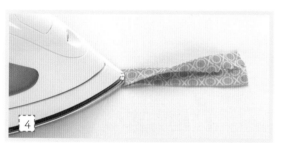

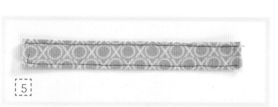

6   Fold the loop in half, overlapping the ends. Pin and baste the loop to the corner of one of the hot pad squares.

7   With the right sides together, stitch the hot pad squares together, leaving an opening for turning. Trim, turn, and press it. Slip-stitch the opening closed.

OVEN MITT

1 For the front and back of the mitt, stitch together six squares—two rows of three squares each.

2 Cut two 11" × 16" (27.9 × 40.6 cm) rectangles of needled, insulated lining. Following the manufacturer's instructions, use spray adhesive to baste the pieced fabric squares to the lining. Topstitch ¼" (6 mm) away from both sides of all seam lines.

3 Enlarge the pattern (page 140) 200% and print it out. Also print the mirror image of the enlarged pattern. Cut two mitts, aligning the pattern lines with the seam lines of each pieced fabric rectangle. Make sure to reverse the pattern so the mitts will line up when sewn right sides together.

4 Cut two 10" × 14" (25.4 × 35.6 cm) rectangles each of lining fabric and fusible fleece. Fuse the fleece to the lining. Place the lining pieces with the fabric sides together and use the pattern to cut the mitt lining pieces.

5 For the front and back of the mitt, place the fleece side of the lining pieces against the insulated side of the mitt outside-fabric pieces. Baste them together ¼" (6 mm) around all edges.

6 Place the front and back of the mitt right sides together and sew from the edge on the thumb side down to the dot on the pattern. Press seam open.

7 As instructed for the pot holder, make the hanger loop from a 5" (12.7 cm) strip. Pin and baste it to one side of the straight side of the mitt, ½" (1.3 cm) from the edge.

8

[11]

8   For the binding, sew a strip to the straight side of the mitt, right sides together. Trim excess fabric from ends and press the seam toward the binding.

9   Placing the right sides together and starting at the point where the stitches ended above the thumb, continue to sew the front of the mitt to the back. Sew across the short ends of the binding strip. Clip the seam at the binding seam line and sew it again ⅛" (.3 mm) into the seam allowance from the previous stitching. Trim excess fabric beyond the second line of stitching.

10   Turn the mitt right side out. You may find it helpful to use the handle of a long wooden spoon to turn out the thumb.

11   Press under the binding seam allowance and slip-stitch over the seam to finish the top edge of the mitt.

MaKE IT YOUrs

- To make the fit of the aprons adjustable, make two neck straps instead of only one, and tie them together at the back of the neck.

- To make half aprons, eliminate the bibs.

- Rickrack and pom-pom trims are optional. You can leave them out or use other types of ribbon and trim that complement the chosen fabrics.

- You can make the pot holder and oven mitt from any combination of strips and squares.

oven mitt
pattern

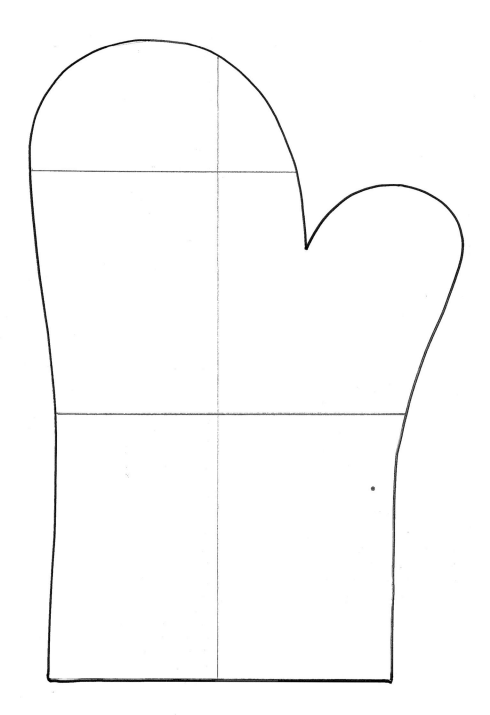

sewing terms glossary

If you are new to sewing or haven't sewn in a while, use this glossary of common sewing terms to refer to as you work on the projects in this book.

BACKSTITCH. To stitch in reverse over the beginning and end of a seam. This action prevents the stitches from unraveling.

BASTE. To temporarily hold fabrics together. Hand or machine basting stitches are very long, straight stitches that you can easily clip and remove. You can also baste with a bit of fabric glue or fusible web.

CLIP. A small cut into the seam allowance to allow the fabric to bend at points and curves. Clipping across the seam allowance of a sewn corner will reduce the bulk of fabric when you turn the project right side out. Take care when clipping not to cut too close or directly into the stitching line.

EDGE-STITCH. To sew a line of stitches very close to a folded edge or seam line.

GATHERING STITCHES. Long machine stitches sewn in one or two rows. When you pull the ends of the threads from both sides of the stitching, the fabric will gather up.

HEM. A turned-under edge. You make it by folding the raw edge of the fabric back inside the project. Use a metal hem gauge and iron to evenly press back the edge to the desired measurement. You make a double hem by folding the raw edge under two times so that no raw edge is visible. The first pressed back fold is what shows on the inside. You can machine-stitch hems close to the inside fold or can hand-sew them with slip stitches. A narrow hem is usually a doubled ¼" (6 mm) hem.

SEAM ALLOWANCE. The distance between the line of stitches and the raw, cut edge of the fabric. When sewing a seam, make sure you align the raw edges. Place them against the guide markings on the sewing machine to assure that you will sew the seam at the desired seam allowance. For narrow seams, the machine's presser foot can serve as the guide.

SELVAGE. The selvage refers to the woven, finished edge of the fabric as it comes off the bolt. The selvage is a bound edge and will not fray. Often the selvage is a contrasting color and contains writing or graphics. You may want to trim the selvage away before working with the fabric. On precut fabrics, you may notice the selvage on one side of a fat quarter and along both short ends of a 2½" (6.4 cm) strip.

SLIP-STITCH. To sew loose hand stitches, catching only a thread of two of fabric. You use slip stitches for securing hems, and they are nearly invisible from the right side of a project.

TRIM. To cut away excess fabric.

TOPSTITCH. To sew a line of stitches on the outside of a project, close to the seam line. You use topstitching for decoration and stability.

ZIGZAG. A machine stitch with a continuous "Z" design. You can sew a zigzag stitch along the raw edge of the fabric to prevent it from fraying.

resources

FABRICS USED IN PROJECTS

- Reversible Table Runner—Westminster Fibers, Free Spirit Designer Essentials, *Subtle Prints*
- Mix and Match Placemats, Napkins and Napkin Rings— Westminster Fibers, Free Spirit, *Wrenly* by Valori Wells
- Patchwork Table Topper—Westminster Fibers, *Blue Classics* by Kaffe Fassett
- Director's Chair Cover—Hoffman Fabrics, Bali Pops Batik Strips, *Key Lime*
- Modern Patchwork Pillow and Lampshade—Fabric Editions, Fabric Palette, *City*
- Window Valance and Pillows—Riley Blake Designs, *Scoot* by Deena Rutter
- Modular Headboard and Accent Pillows—Sheri Berry Designs, *Mod-Tod* by Riley Blake
- Tea Cozy, Trivet, and Towel—Hoffman Fabrics, Bali Pops Batik Strips, *Watermelon*
- Pretty Pleated Purse—Riley Blake Designs, *So Sophie* by My Mind's Eye
- Reversible Tote and Clutch Bag—Westminster Fibers, *Neutral Classics* by Kaffe Fassett
- Hobo Bag—Westminster Fibers, *Red Classics* by Kaffe Fassett
- Easy, Breezy Little Girl's Dress—Fabric Editions, Fabric Palette, *Flutterby-Pink*
- Roll and Ruffle Skirt—Westminster Fibers, Free Spirit, *Taza* by Dena Designs
- Snuggle Blanket and Soft Blocks—Westminster Fibers, Free Spirit Designer Essentials, *Soft Prints*
- I Love Sleepovers Duffle Bag and Pillow Case—Westminster Fibers, Free Spirit , Designer Essentials, *Bold prints*
- Bargello Yoga Mat Bag—Westminster Fibers, *Green Classics* by Kaffe Fassett
- Tisket Tasket Fabric Basket—Westminster Fibers, Free Spirit, *Blossoming* by Kathy Davis
- Mommy and Me Aprons, Pot Holder, and Oven Mitt—Westminster Fibers, Free Spirit, *LouLouThi* by Anna Maria Horner

SEWING AND CRAFTING SUPPLIES

Contact the following manufacturers for fabrics and supplies used to make the projects in this book.

Beacon Adhesives
Fabri-Tac fabric glue
www.beaconadhesives.com

Coats & Clark
Dual Duty XP General Purpose sewing thread
www.coatsandclark.com

Fairfield Processing
Fiberfill, pillow inserts, batting
www.fairfieldworld.com

Fasturn LLC
Fasturn™ tools for turning fabric tubes
www.fasturn.net

Fiskars
Sewing and quilting scissors
www.fiskars.com

Imaginisce
i-top tool for fabric-covered buttons
www.imaginisce.com

Making Memories
Slice Fabrique™
www.whyslice.com

Pellon
Batting, interfacing, fleece, stabilizers
www.pellon.ca

Dritz/Prym Consumer USA
Omnigrid ruler and cutting mats; Dritz rotary cutters and sewing notions
www.dritz.com

ODIF USA
Spray and fix adhesives for fabric
www.odifusa.com

Renaissance Ribbons
Woven jacquard designer ribbons
www.renaissanceribbons.com

Roc-lon
Multi-purpose cloth™
www.roc-lon.com

Rowley
Perfect Pleating Tape
www.rowleycompany.com

Simplicity Creative Group
Simplicity bias tape maker and rotary cutting machine
www.simplicity.com

Sizzix
Big Shot die-cutting machine
www.sizzix.com

The Warm Company
Insul-Bright™ insulated lining, Steam-A-Seam™ fusible web
www.warmcompany.com

ABOUT THE AUTHOR

Elaine Schmidt, of Long Valley, New Jersey, is a designer, consultant, educator, and spokesperson in the sewing, quilting, and craft industries. She works with leading creative industry manufacturers to develop new products, inspire their consumers, and promote innovative uses for their products.

Elaine is a fabric addict, ribbon hoarder, button and bead collector, yarn and thread junkie, and sewing geek who grew up always making something. Brought up learning proper, traditional sewing techniques by her mom, she now enjoys bending the old-school rules a bit and "coloring outside the lines." Never happy to do one thing at a time, Elaine always has several projects going.

Elaine's love of sewing led her to major in textiles and design at Carnegie Mellon University. She has worked in the education and design departments of a major sewing pattern company and is the former design director for a national chain of ribbon boutiques. Elaine recently authored *The Complete Photo Guide to Ribbon Crafts* for Quayside Publishing. As the owner of Elaine Schmidt Designs, she has developed award-winning products for many manufacturers. Books, magazines, websites, project sheets, and TV segments as well as national trade and consumer sewing, quilting and craft shows feature her original designs.

You can catch up on her latest inspirations and projects by visiting her blog at https://elaineschmidt.wordpress.com

ACKNOWLEDGMENTS

To my wonderful husband Kenny, my sounding board, my IT guy, my biggest cheerleader, my partner in life, and my best friend. Thank you for your constant love and support that have allowed me to always do the things I like to do.

And to our daughters, Elizabeth, Emily, and Carlee. As our family grows, I know we will always be close in spirit and heart, despite the miles apart.

To my family members and many friends who are a constant source of encouragement and strength.

To Linda Neubauer and the staff at Quayside Publishing. Thank you for believing in me and giving me the opportunity to work on another book with you.

To the many manufacturers who so generously supported me with product samples and information. It's easy to make great projects when you work with quality products.

And a very special memorial to my mother, Irene Turansky. Although you never got to see this book finished, you were with me in each stitch I sewed and each word I wrote. Not only did you teach me how to sew, you taught me how to live a life of love and faith and giving to others. I know you are up in heaven now, probably busy at your sewing machine designing robes for the angels or repairing their wings. Sleep warm. I'll always love and remember you.

ANOTHER GREAT BOOK FROM ELANIE SCHMIDT!

The Complete Photo Guide to Ribbon Crafts
Elaine Schmidt
978-1-58923-469-7

ALSO AVAILABLE FROM CREATIVE PUBLISHING INTERNATIONAL!

Playful Patchwork
Suzuko Koseki
978-1-58923-605-9

Quilting 101
978-1-58923-473-4

Sewing Clothes Kids Love
Nancy Langdon and
Sabine Pollehn
978-1-58923-473-4

The Complete Photo Guide to Sewing
978-1-5923-434-5

OUR BOOKS ARE AVAILABLE AS E-BOOKS, TOO!

Many of our bestselling titles are now available as E-Books.
Visit www.Qbookshop.com to find links to e-vendors!

Available online or at your
local craft or book store.

www.creativepub.com

Creative Publishing
international